Guinea Fowl

Guinea Fowl as pets

Guinea Fowl Keeping, Pros and Cons, Care, Housing, Diet and Health.

by

Roger Rodendale

Contents

Introduction...6

Chapter 1: Meet the Guinea Fowl **8**

    a. Appearance of the Guinea Fowl *8*

    b. Taxonomy.. *10*

    c. Distribution and Habitat................................... *15*

    d. History of the Guinea Fowl................................ *16*

    e. Behavior *17*

    f. Food Habits *18*

Chapter 2: Your First Guinea **20**

    a. Considerations before getting your Guinea Fowl *20*

    b. Why do you want Guinea Fowl?............................. *22*

    c. Types of Rearing Systems *24*

    d. What are the best options to buy your birds?................ *25*

    e. How old should the bird be?................................ *29*

Chapter 3: Progression of Guinea Fowl **32**

    a. Preparing for Keets... *32*

    b. First two weeks... *34*

    c. White Millet Taming *35*

    d. Moving them to the Coop................................... *36*

    e. Perching... *37*

    f. At 6 weeks *38*

    g. Ready to free range *38*

Chapter 4: Managing your Guineas **41**

Table of Contents

a. Coop management.. 41

b. Make space 42

c. Managing different birds.. 43

d. Guinea Fowl and other Pets 46

e. To pinion or not to pinion 48

f. Flock behavior of Guinea Fowl 51

Chapter 5: Raising your Guinea Fowl **54**

a. What to feed them 54

b. Types of feeders available 57

c. Housing a Guinea.. 59

d. Building a coop... 64

e. Keeping the coop clean.. 67

f. Managing predators 69

g. Transporting Guinea Fowl 76

Chapter 6: Breeding and Incubation **79**

a. Sexing the Guinea Fowl 79

b. Managing breeding flocks... 81

c. Production of eggs... 82

d. Hatching the eggs 83

e. Incubating the eggs... 84

Chapter 7: Common Guinea Fowl Diseases **95**

a. Signs of illnesses in Guinea Fowl 95

b. Respiratory illnesses 97

c. Non Respiratory illnesses... 100

d. Behavioral problems in Guinea Fowl...................................... 105

Table of Contents

e. Veterinary Care... 107

f. First Aid and Preventive Care 109

g. Insurance for Guinea Fowl.. 113

Conclusion **116**

References...**117**

Introduction

Guinea Fowl are among the least known birds for domestic rearing. Most people would believe that these birds are actually Turkeys. While they have a close resemblance to these popular farm birds, Guinea Fowl are very unique birds that are known for their awkward yet puckish nature.

One of the most commonly found species of the Guinea Fowl is the "Helmeted pearl". These beautiful polka dotted birds are reared as pets and sometimes for meat. For those who rear Guinea Fowl, they are the best source of entertainment as they scuttle around and simply love to forage through the soil.

There are many other reasons why Guinea Fowl make wonderful pets. They are especially popular on farms because they usually keep predators that eat chicken and turkey away. On ranches, these birds are usually kept to keep deadly snakes like copperheads and rattle snakes away. Of course, in the urban set up, these birds eat up most disease carrying pets. Besides that, they keep birds that destroy flowers and plants away and also keep farms free from any weed and insects. It is no wonder that these birds are kept in large numbers by people who want to make farming and poultry rearing a lucrative business. According to Cindy Gibson, President of Guinea Fowl International, these birds have become popular primarily because of their ability to keep bugs and ticks at bay.

These birds are a delight to first time fowl owners because they are low maintenance. Since these birds are not really reared for eggs or meat they have not fallen prey to hybridization. That makes them very hardy and highly resistant to diseases. They can also thrive in just about any kind of climatic conditions. And, the fact that these birds will always thrive in groups or pairs makes them hard for predators to get to as well. In short, these birds are a delight to have around if you do not know much about caring for birds.

Now, that said, it does not mean that you can just buy these birds and let them loose in your backyard and watch them grow. They have their own share of requirements that you need to focus on if you want to raise healthy birds in your home. You need to make sure that the birds are protected irrespective of their resistance to diseases and predators. You also need to pay a lot of attention to the nutritional requirements of these birds. These are the things that you need to learn before you bring Guinea Fowl home.

This book gives you all the information that you will need to provide the right care for your Guinea Fowl. You will also learn about the pros and cons of having these birds in your home, helping you make an informed decision about actually choosing them as pets.

One thing that you can be certain about when you opt for Guinea Fowl is that you are in for a lot of adventures and laughs thanks to these "little grey men".

Chapter 1: Meet the Guinea Fowl

The Guinea Fowl, which are also known as "Gleanies", are very important birds on farmlands and other agricultural set ups. Their ability to keep pests at bay is one of the most important reasons for the growing popularity of the bird. Now, the only problem with this bird is the inability of new owners to identify these birds. Most often they are confused with Turkeys. If you are going for a Guinea Fowl and bring home a Turkey instead, you are not only going to pay more for the bird but are also going to have a hard time raising them. This chapter will tell you everything that you need to know about the appearance, behavior and other general things about the Guinea Fowl to make sure that you do not have any unfortunate experiences.

a. Appearance of the Guinea Fowl

There are different species of the Guinea Fowl of which the Helmeted Guinea Fowl is the most commonly domesticated one. This bird is plump in its appearance and is close to a chicken in size. They have a sort of humped back physique. The distinguishing physical feature of these birds are the slate grey plumes covering the body of the birds. These feathers have several white dots on them that almost look like polka dots.

The neck of the Guinea Fowl is short and does not have any feathers. Even the head is featherless and has a casque that looks like a scimitar. This body structure gives the Helmeted Guinea Fowl its name. The lower face and the upper neck have a characteristic sky blue colored skin. The wattles are red tipped while the throat flap is a darker shade of blue.

The forehead, cere and the crown of the bird are red in color while the casque and the bill are horn colored. The iris of the Guinea Fowl is brown. There are some small feathers on the lower neck that look almost like down feathers. These feathers are brownish grey in color and will extend almost half way up the back of the bird's upper neck. As these feathers go lower, they merge with the slate grey plumage of the bird. Each of these feathers will have uniformly placed white dots that give the bird a speckled look.

The flight feathers of the bird also look similar to the body feathers. The only difference is that these feathers have lines on the outer web. The dots merge in this region to form these lines which remain aligned while the bird's wings are closed. So, it has a barred look.

Domesticated Guinea Fowl tend to have whitish skin on the face. Sometimes, they may also have white colored flight feathers and some patches of white on the belly and the flanks. The legs of the bird are dark grey in color in the wild Guinea Fowl. If the birds have been domesticated, the feet are usually orange. There are no leg spurs.

The male and female birds have very few differences in the physical appearance. The casque in the females is narrower and shorter. Even the wattles in these birds are smaller. The only major distinguishing factor between the male and the female is the call. We will talk about the sounds of the Guinea Fowl in the following chapters. Juvenile birds are also very similar to the adults. Only the facial skin is paler and the spots are not as well developed as the adults. As for the chicks, they have brownish grey feathers with black fringes. The flight feathers look the same too. The feathers on the head are brown and have vertical black stripes.

These physical appearances should be given a lot of importance not only to make sure that you are bringing the right bird home but to also ensure that you are bringing a healthy bird home.

Guinea Fowl Facts: As mentioned before, the Guinea Fowl look very similar to juvenile wild Turkeys or even the adult female Turkeys. The casque is the most important distinguishing factor between the two birds. In addition to that the plumes on the body of the Turkey do not have any dots on them.

b. Taxonomy

Guinea Fowl belong to the order *Galliformes* that consists of other poultry birds like chickens and turkeys as well. These birds are classified in the family *Numididae*. There are four genera of these birds that are further divided into a total of six species.

Genus Aglestes: There are two species under this genus:

The White Breasted Guinea Fowl or *Aglestes megleagrrides*

This species consists of medium sized birds that grow up to 45 cm in length. They are terrestrial birds that have a very typical black plumage with a long black tail. The head is bare and red in color. The white breast of this bird is the most striking feature that also gives the bird its name. The bill is greenish brown in color while the feet are greyish in color. The females are smaller than the male birds. Besides that, there are not differentiating characteristics as such.

These birds are typically found in the sub-tropical regions of West Africa in the forests of Ghana, Liberia, Sierra Leone and Cote d'loire. These birds are omnivorous with a diet that consists of termites, berries, a few smaller animals and seeds.

These birds have been listed by the IUCN as a vulnerable species. The constant loss of habitat and hunting of these birds in some regions have depleted the numbers of these birds quite rapidly, putting them in the danger of becoming extinct.

The Black Guinea Fowl or *The Agelastes niger*

The Black Guinea Fowl is yet another medium sized bird. The head is not feathered and has a pinkish appearance. The forehead and the crown have a crest that consists of short feathers. These feathers scatter down to the lower neck. The plumage of the body is fully black with a few paler and specked feathers near the belly.

The legs of the male have between 1 and 3 spurs while the females may not have any or perhaps just one short spur. Juvenile birds look quite similar to the adult birds. However, the feathers will have buff tips on the upper parts. The belly is white while the feathers on the breast are speckled.

The beak of these birds is greyish green and the legs are greyish brown. The other distinguishing factor between the males and the females is the size. The females are smaller in size and are also lighter than the males.

These birds are found in the West Central African region including Cameroon, Equatorial guinea, Angola, Gabon, Nigeria and the Central African republic. They are usually found on the forest floor of the tropical rainforests.

These birds mainly feed on ants, millipedes, termites and beetles. They even eat smaller animals like frogs. Their diet includes shoots, berries and roots as well. Although these birds have been placed under the Least Concern category by the IUCN, their numbers are depleting because of habitat loss and hunting for game.

Very little is known about the behavior of these birds. They are very shy and elusive creatures that are mostly seen in small groups or pairs. They like to be in areas that have thick undergrowth so that they are not spotted easily. One main problem with these birds is that they venture into the cultivated areas nearby and are seen as pests.

Genus Numida

Helmeted Guinea Fowl or *Numida meleagris*

These are the most common domesticated Guinea Fowl. They are naïve to Africa, in the Sahara region. These birds are recognized by the speckled plumage. There are nine subspecies of these birds that are classified based on the habitat. The nine subspecies are:

- *Numida meleagris coronatus* or the Helmeted Guinea Fowl that has its origins in the eastern part of South Africa.
- *Numida meleagris geleatus* or the West African Guinea Fowl that hails from the Western part of Africa including, Central Zaire, North Angola and Chad.
- *Numida meleagris marungenesis* or the Marungu Helmeted Guinea Fowl that hails from the South Congo Basin.
- *Numida meleagris meleagris* or the Saharan Helmeted Guinea Fowl that are found in the eastern region from Chad to Ethiopia, Kenya, Uganda and Zaire.
- *Numida meleagris mitratus* or the tufted Guinea Fowl that originate in the range from Tanzania to Zambia, Northern Botswana and Mozambique.
- *Numida meleagris papillosus* or the Damara Helmeted Guinea Fowl that are found in Botswana, Southern Angola and Namibia.
- *Numida meleagris reichenowi* or the Reichenow's Helmeted Guinea Fowl that is found in Central Tanzania and Kenya
- *Numida meleagris sabyi* or the Saby's Helmeted Guinea Fowl that originates from Northwester Morocco.
- *Numida meleagris somaliensis* or The Somali Tufted Guinea Fowl that is found in Somalia and North Eastern Ethiopia.

These birds are known for making great pets and watchdogs and are growing in popularity across the world.

Genus Guttera

Plumed Guinea Fowl or *Guttera Plumifera*

This bird is primarily found in Central Africa in the humid forests. It is very similar in appearance to the crested Guinea Fowl. However, the shape of the crest is the distinguishing factor. The crest of this Guinea Fowl is higher and straighter unlike the Crested Guinea Fowl which has a curved crest. The wattle is relatively longer in case of the Plumed Guinea Fowl. It is seen quite conspicuously on the either side of the beak. The skin on the face and neck are bare and have a dull bluish grey appearance. This is in case of the Western Subspecies of the Guinea Fowl. The Easter subspecies will also have orange patches on this grey skin.

There are two sub species:

- The Cameroon Plumed Guinea Fowl or the *Guttera Plumifera plumifera* are native to north Angola, north Gabon, south Cameroon and the Congo Basin.
- The Shubotz' Plumed Guinea Fowl or the *Guttera Plumifera schubotzi* are found in the Eastern African Rift, North Zaireand the forests around Lake Taganyika

These birds have been classified as Least Concern in the IUCN Red List. Their diet consists of seeds, insects and a few smaller animals.

The Crested Guinea Fowl or the *Guttera Pucherani*

Found mostly in the open forests and savanna regions of the sub Saharan range of Africa, these birds are large with very specific physical characteristics. The plumes of this bird are black overall and consist of white spots that are very densely placed. The crest of the bird is definitely the most striking feature. It is seen on the top of the head in the form of curly feathers or soft down feathers, depending upon the subspecies of the bird. This crest helps you distinguish this bird from the other Guinea Fowl.

There are five subspecies of this bird:

- *Guttera Pucherani barbata* or the Malawi Crested Guinea Fowl which is native to Malawi, South Eastern Tanzania and Eastern Mozambique.
- *Guttera Pucherani eduoardi* which is found in the region between Mozambique and Eastern Zambia. It is also found in the eastern part of South Africa.
- *Guttera Pucherani pucherani* or the Kenya Crested Guinea Fowl which is found between Tanzania and Somalia and parts of the Tumbatu Island and Zanzibar.
- *Guttera Pucherani sclateri* or the Scalter's Crested Guinea Fowl which are normally found in the north western region of Cameroon.
- *Guttera Pucherani verreauxi* or the Lindi Crested Guinea Fowl which is found in Western Kenya, Zambia and Angola.

Genus Acryllium

Vulturine Guinea Fowl or *Acryllium vulturinum*
They are closest related to the White Breasted Guinea Fowl. It is found in the North-eastern part of Africa and in the region from Southern Ethiopia extending to Kenya and a part of the northern region of Tanzania.

These are large birds that have a small head and a well-rounded body. The wings, legs, neck and tail of these birds are the longest among all types of Guinea Fowl. The face of an adult Vulturine Guinea Fowl is blue in color and is bare. The neck is black in color. Like vultures, all Guinea Fowl have a bare head. However, this one looks more like a vulture because of the long neck.

The slim neck extends into the hackles that are blue and glossy. The breast of the Vulturine Guinea Fowl is a striking cobalt blue color. The rest of the body consists of black plumes with white spangles. The wings are rounded and short while the tail is long. The females are smaller in size as compared to the males. The younger birds are usually grey brown in color. They have very short hackles and will also have duller plumage on the breast.

These birds tend to live in large flocks going up to 25 birds. This is not even in the breeding season. They are just extremely gregarious birds. They are terrestrial birds that tend to run instead of flying when they are alarmed. Though the habitat of this bird includes open areas, it tends to stay covered and mostly roosts in the trees.

These birds can only breed when they have scattered bushes like the open habitats of Africa. They need dry conditions in order to thrive well. Their diet mostly consists of small insects and seeds.

These are all the species and sub species of the Guinea Fowl. However, if you are interested in raising and domesticating these birds, it is the Helmeted Guinea Fowl that will be of maximum interest to you. These birds are easily available, hardy and of course most domesticated in comparison to all the other wild species of the Numididae Family.

c. Distribution and Habitat

These birds are normally found in the Sub Saharan Regions of Africa. They occupy almost the entire range. Some of the sub species like the Plumed Guinea Fowl and the Vulturine Guinea Fowl are more localized species. Most of these birds are found in open grasslands and scrubs of Africa. Some of them, like the black Guinea Fowl, are found on the forest floors. These birds like to stay under cover and will only roost in concealed areas. When reared extensively, these birds need to perch on tall trees in order to survive and feel secure.

The Helmeted Guinea Fowl has been introduced in various parts of the world including The USA, Britain, Australia, New Zealand and India. In these areas, they are raised as pets or are raised for food.

Populations of these birds decline rapidly in areas where pesticides are commonly used. The distribution of these birds in other parts of the world excluding Africa is mainly attributed to escapes from domestic setups. In some parts of the world, such as the Whanganui region of New Zealand, these birds are unable to sustain themselves naturally and tend to diminish despite several deliberate re-introductions.

d. History of the Guinea Fowl

The Guinea Fowl originated in Africa. However, they have been domesticated across the world for several years. In fact, drawings of their birds on the walls of the pyramid suggest how early people began to welcome these birds into their homes.

As we discussed before, there are several varieties of Guinea Fowl that have sprung up over the years because of cross breeding among species. In some countries, these birds remain popular game birds just like the Partridge or the Pheasant in the United Kingdom. But when did the domestication of these birds begin and how did they become so popular globally?

These birds have been quite an important part of our history. Along with the jungle fowl, these birds formed very easy game birds that could be captured or killed quite easily. It is believed that as the African tribes progressed towards agricultural habitats from pastoral ones, these birds were domesticated too.

Sir Harry Johnston, a popular British explorer, states that the Ancient Egyptians reared these birds along with red-legged Partridges and Francolin as curiosities. Small statuettes of these birds have been found, dating back to over 4000 years ago. That is proof that these birds were raised in captivity for so many centuries. However, the Egyptians were not responsible for these becoming an integral part of the modern poultry yards, ranches and farms.

These birds are found in big numbers in Kordofan, Sudan. These birds have a nick name in this region which is *Abu Konan.* This is also an alternative name for the Arab inhabitants who lived in the northern parts of this region. It is believed that these birds were given the name because of their close relationship with these people. In fact, it is believed that these birds were originally domesticated poultry that were kept and bred by the aboriginal people of this area.

However, when their masters abandoned the birds or migrated from these areas, these birds also began to run wild. These birds, it is believed, were extremely large in size and were often considered giant chickens.

These birds were first brought to the Western part of Europe in the 16th century. They were brought in as great game birds. Soon, these birds gained popularity also because of their eggs that were considered extremely tasty. Today, these birds can also be found in large numbers in the wild. In Rome, especially, the eggs and the meat of these birds were considered to be delicacies.

In the 1500s, after the arrival of Christopher Colombus in the United States of America, the Spanish brought these birds to the Americas. Today, there are several breeders who have worked on hybridizing the bird to form various colors and varieties of this species.

It is hard to state the exact population of these birds across the globe simply because large populations seem to disappear from certain parts of the world, especially New Zealand. Of course, what you can be certain of is the fact that their population spreads across several continents including Asia, the Americas, Australia, Europe and of course, Africa.

e. Behavior

In the wild these birds are usually seen in groups of about 7-20 birds. They love to walk around, forage, peck at the ground and even scratch the ground just like chickens. They tend to keep calling as they move forth. The males are more playful or aggressive in some cases. They tend to chase one another around, trying to claim hierarchy over the group. But, these birds are rather gentle and you will rarely see them breaking into a proper fight.

When they are foraging, these birds like to stay in areas where they are covered. They are rather shy and elusive in their behavior. If they are alarmed, they will rarely fly and will choose to run instead. Sometimes when they are really threatened, these birds will burst into a steep fight. They have a shrill alarming call the goes like this *"kekkekkekkkek"*. However, do not assume that these birds do not fly. They are very strong flyers. They have dark breast muscles that give them the strength that they need to sustain flight. They fly over long distances when required. Forest fires and bush fires are common reasons in the wild that make these birds migrate and use their power of flying.

In a domestic set up, you will notice that these birds are very different from the regular poultry animals. They are a lot more active and are not so easy to tame. Catching Guinea Fowl, it is said, is a lot harder than catching chickens.

These birds come with a very strong personality which makes them a little tricky to keep with other poultry birds. They tend to get aggressive even with new Guinea Fowl introduced to their flock. Sometimes, the new bird can be extremely aggressive too. These birds tend to be extremely territorial. If someone enters their territory they will make sharp and rather disturbing calls.

This personality also makes these birds wonderful farm animals. They are great watchdogs and can actually ward off most predators because of their strength as a flock.

These birds are quite adorable according to most owners. They are never aggressive towards people and will always mind their own business when given enough space to move around and exercise. These birds are really entertaining and you can spend almost the whole day just watching them busy in their pursuit of worms and snails.

f. Food Habits

In the wild, Guinea Fowl are omnivorous creatures. They usually eat grass seeds, leaves, vegetable matter and fruits. They usually prefer eating smaller invertebrates. These birds are equipped with

18

very strong legs that allow them to grub out food like beetles, bugs, bulbs and seedlings from the ground. They occasionally enjoy eating insect larvae, flower heads, fruits of certain herbaceous plants and bugs.

They may also eat frogs, small lizards ad mice occasionally. They use their strong bills to kill their prey. One interesting thing to watch in the wild is these birds jumping up to a few centimetres to pluck flowers or fruits from bushes.

Chapter 2: Your First Guinea

Guinea Fowl are extremely low maintenance, no doubt. However, these birds are not the easiest to tame. They also tend to be rather noisy. So before you bring your Guinea Fowl home, here are a few things that you need to know.

a. Considerations before getting your Guinea Fowl

There is no doubting the fact that Guinea Fowl make wonderful pets. They are great watchdogs, are pleasant around human beings and can be quite fun to have around. However, if this is your first time with Guinea Fowl, there are a few things that you need to consider and understand. You definitely do not want to have any unexpected surprises that may make you want to abandon the birds in the future.

- They are low maintenance but they do come with the basic requirements. Guinea Fowl are a financial commitment. Just like any other pet, you will have to provide them with food, shelter and healthcare. Making sure that they are clean and healthy also requires time. You cannot just let the birds forage and roost in trees but will have to shop for fresh greens and make sure that they have a warm shelter every night.
- In comparison to chickens, Guinea Fowl are less destructive. But they do scratch the ground and may end up damaging some of your plants and property. This is something you need to be prepared for. To make sure that they do not go rampant on your flowerbed for their dusting needs you need to give them some sort of sandy area or dirt pit.
- Guinea Fowl can wander really far. They are also rather boisterous creatures that are not afraid of vehicles and predators. So, if you have clipped the wings of your bird or live close to the main road with traffic, it is likely that you will lose a few of your birds. Now that is pretty heart breaking but even fencing cannot hold these adventurous little creatures back.

- Guinea Fowl tend to go missing in the egg laying season. They tend to help each other brood the eggs. Sometimes, your female guineas may even come back home with other babies. You need to prevent this from happening and make sure that you give your Guinea Fowl a separate area to brood in so that they do not mix with the other females.

- We mentioned before that Guinea Fowl are very effective at keeping predators at bay. That, however, doesn't mean that they are safe from predators. The young ones especially are susceptible to attacks. It is common for Guinea Fowl to be under threat for at least 1 year. At this age, they are not really equipped to handle a surprise attack. So you need to make sure that you give them enough space to cover themselves, including long grass or even shrubs that they can hide under.

- You need to prepare for the changing seasons. While Guinea Fowl are quite hardy, they do not do very well in snow. They simply dislike it. You need to make sure that you have paths shoveled out for your guineas. And, if it gets too cold, you may have to provide the birds with an alternate source of heat and light. Even the water may need a heater if it needs to be good enough for the birds.

- Getting rid of predators is very expensive. If you have had any predator attacks in your home in the past, there is nothing else you can do but get the house fortified. You need to always keep your Guinea Fowl safe even though they are known to ward off predators very well.

- If you already have birds at home such as chickens or ducks, introducing Guinea Fowl is a lot of work. You must always be prepared to provide the birds with separate spaces of their own if you want to make sure that they are safe. Sometimes they get along but most often, they just don't!

- The pecking order establishment is definitely very harsh among these birds. If you are a first time owner, this can get very overwhelming if you are not prepared for it. Birds may fight hard, and end up injured or dead. If you notice that one of the male guineas is being very aggressive, you must have the necessary space to isolate the bird. Then, you can only hope that some other male takes the dominant place in a peaceful manner forcing the former to behave well.

- Guinea Fowl can be cruel birds. If one of them is unwell or has any deformity, they will shun the bird. In that case, the birds only do this to ensure that the flock is safe. But that puts the onus on you to make sure that the bird is safe. You will have to give him a spot in the coop where he can hide in case the dominant males get too aggressive.

What you need to really know as a Guinea Fowl owner is that these birds are less demanding in comparison to chickens and other poultry birds. But what no one tells you is that they still need to be given a lot of attention. You will have to always work towards the health and safety of these birds.

As a Guinea Fowl owner, you need to be prepared to constantly learn more about the birds, try to understand flock behavior and make sure that you do not neglect any small change in behavior. If you are able to give your little flock time, you can bring one home. Of course, these birds are a big financial commitment, especially because you need to care for multiple birds.

b. Why do you want Guinea Fowl?

There are several reasons why people want to bring Guinea Fowl home. Depending on what your needs are, the way you rear them, the kind of training that you need to give them etc. will change depending upon why you want to bring these birds home. Here are some common reasons why people bring home these birds:

Great watch dogs

When something unfamiliar approaches your home or property, you can expect a lot of noise and commotion from these birds. They have a very specific alarm call that will tell you that there is a predator or an intruder in your home. If you plan to bring them home to take care of your home, it is a good idea to bring them home as a group. That way, you know that they will be safer. Guinea Fowl will just go after an intruder and may get injured seriously without a flock to protect them.

Nutritious meat and eggs

Guinea Fowl produce eggs seasonally unlike chickens. In addition to that, their eggs are not even large. However, these eggs are highly nutritious because of which many people grow Guinea Fowl. The meat is also very sought after and is considered a delicacy in America and Europe. This is because their meat is much lower in cholesterol and richer in flavor when compared to chicken meat. The meat is dark and extremely delicate. If you are raising them for eggs or meat, you need a really large number to make it sustainable.

Sustainable lifestyle

Guinea Fowl are a farmer or gardener's best friend. This is because they make sure that other farm animals are protected. In many cases, the farm animals contract deadly diseases from the poultry. This is a very big issue faced by farmers. Of course, their manure also makes the soil very rich in nutrients promoting better farming. Their manure is usually composted even when they are not commercially reared because of the quality. This manure can be composted and even used in a home garden for better growth of all the plants.

Pest Control

These birds, when kept in flocks, are known for their work as a team. They will eat most of the pets that can ruin your farm or your garden. But, the good news is that they will not ruin the plants in your garden while doing so. They are foragers, no doubt. In addition to this, these birds are free rangers. This means that they will look for pests all over your property. They hunt down common pests like grasshoppers, fleas, snakes, crickets and even beetles. If you have been facing an issue with pests, you may opt for Guinea Fowl as a natural remedy. These birds are fun to watch, can provide good manure and will also prevent the use of harmful chemicals. In farms, especially, this is a great advantage as the produce is organic and free from any possible chemical.

Entertainment

Of course, there are many who just want to bring Guinea Fowl home for entertainment or ornamental purposes. As mentioned before, these birds can make great pets as they keep themselves busy with almost clownish activities. In addition to that, hybridization has led to several colors and feather patterns that make these birds great for ornamental purposes. Some of the common colors of Guinea Fowl include royal purple, lavender and blue. These curious birds are very pleasant to be around. They are also good around human beings and will mingle with most people quite easily, making wonderful pets for all. If you are bringing them home just as pets, you will have to work on training them to behave. It is a good idea to start with a pair of birds and then move on to a flock. If you are adopting or bringing home an adult bird, it is recommended that you only opt for a well bonded pair. That will make it easier for you to handle the birds and you won't have to go through the hassle of introducing these birds to one another.

Although Guinea Fowl are a great responsibility, the advantages of keeping these birds at home make all the efforts worth it. They are among the most easily maintained pets ever. When you are bringing Guinea Fowl home, be very careful about the purpose. If you know why you want a new pet, you will know whether you want to opt for Guinea Fowl or any other species of birds that are available. This decision will also determine the rearing system that you will opt for. There are three popular systems that you can choose from depending upon convenience and the need.

c. Types of Rearing Systems

These are three major rearing systems for Guinea Fowl depending upon the purpose of the birds and their role in your home. In some agricultural communities, these birds are reared collectively and kept in good health because of the several benefits of having these birds around. You can choose from one of the following rearing systems once you have figured out why you want Guinea Fowl in your home:

Free Range Rearing System
This is the most commonly practiced rearing system in Africa. In many countries where the farmers do not have access to too many resources, Guinea Fowl play a major role in agriculture. You will see this form of rearing in most developing countries. It makes farming sustainable and actually has great economic value. They normally involve rural communities that take up the provision of drinking water for the birds and also ensure that their health always remains protected.

Semi Free Rearing System
This is perhaps the best rearing system if you are not commercially raising the birds but have them at home only for ornamental purposes or as pets. This is when you will have separate housing for your bird and will also allow them to free range around your garden or backyard. Now, with this type of rearing, you will have to take a lot of precautions. You need to make sure that they are safe. This will require fencing and also pinioning of the birds. This makes sure that they do not fly away or wander too far away.

Intensive Rearing System
This system of rearing is used by people who are rearing Guinea Fowl for commercial purposes. These birds are not given any access to the outdoors and will be kept in certain types of coops that alternate between light and darkness. The main purpose of this kind of rearing is to ensure that the birds have better performance. They are raised to breed in the soil or in special batteries. Now, in the modern systems of rearing these birds, they are artificially inseminated and are reared in batteries to make sure that they produce more eggs. This is feasible only if the birds are going to be marketed and used commercially.

d. What are the best options to buy your birds?
You have several options to obtain your Guinea Fowl from. The number and the purpose of the birds matters when you choose the source of your Guinea Fowl. The common options include:

Breeders

There are several breeders who can help you obtain healthy birds for your home. The advantage with breeders is that they do not produce these birds only for egg production and meat. So, if you are interested in rearing Guinea Fowl for ornamentation or for shows, it is a good idea to look for a breeder. The Guinea Fowl International Association has a list of breeders in various countries that breed healthy birds.

You can get birds that are as young as just 1 day old. If you plan to buy from a breeder, give him or her a call and ask when the next batch would be ready. Based on that you can fix an appointment to meet the breeder and take a thorough look at the space that they own. This visit is crucial as it will help you figure out if your breeder is selling healthy birds or not. Normally, three color varieties of birds are available with the breeders including:

- The pearl variety: This is the most common one that is easy to recognize. Most people only identify these birds. Their feathers are purplish-grey in color. They have several white spots on the body that almost look like pearls, hence the name. These birds are commonly brought home for ornamental purposes.
- The lavender variety: These birds are very similar to the pearl variety. The only difference is that the plumage is lighter and almost look lavender instead of purple. They also have white spots like the pearl guineas.
- African white variety: These birds will have pure white feathers. They have no spots on the plumes. One thing you need to know about these birds is that they are not an albino version of the regular Guinea Fowl.

Guinea Fowl Facts: The African White Guinea Fowl are the only white birds with white hatchlings. All other white birds have yellow hatchlings that later turn white.

When you go to a breeder, make sure you pick one that is experienced with Guinea Fowl. It is a good idea to ask for recommendations from other Guinea Fowl owners. However, you can be pretty sure that you are buying from a genuine breeder when you choose one from the Guinea Fowl International Association.

It is a good idea to meet your breeder in person and take a look at the conditions of the coop. They should be able to provide you with all the information that you need with respect to nutrition and care of the bird.

Take a close look at the birds when you are there. Guinea Fowl are normally very active and edgy birds. If you see that the Guinea Fowl that you are going to buy look lethargic and do not move around much, it is an indication of poor health. The feces is also a giveaway with respect to the bird's health. Normally, a healthy Guinea Fowl's feces is not as unpleasant as other poultry birds like chickens. However, if the coop smells really bad, it is an indication of health problems within the flock.

There are online breeders as well. Most of them are reliable. However, there are chances that you will end up with birds that are unwell or even dead when they are shipped. It is best that you find a breeder locally to collect the birds and make sure that they are healthy.

Hatcheries
Usually hatcheries are opted for by people who want to bring home Guinea Fowl for eggs or for meat. You can either choose to buy eggs or the keets from a hatchery. They will most likely ship a box of the birds to a post office close to you. These hatcheries produce hundreds of chicks and are spread across a country. They have a minimum order most of the time. With Guinea Fowl, you need to order a minimum of three from a breeder usually.

At hatcheries, these birds are usually bred for good egg production and not so much for their appearance. So, if you are looking for show birds, this is not the best option to obtain your bird from. You can even buy juvenile birds from these hatcheries. These birds are typically 15-22 weeks of age.

Unless you are ordering, you can check the gender of the bird that you are going to obtain from the hatchery. That way you can have an even flock with the same number of males and females. The only issue with hatcheries is that when you are having them shipped it is very stressful until they finally arrive.

Now, if you are getting eggs from your breeder or hatchery but do not know what color you want them to be, you have the option of ordering a "Rainbow Layer". This is a collection of eggs from birds of different colors. So, when they hatch you have all the varieties.

Other options

Adoption is a great option if you want to bring home adult Guinea Fowl. You have the option of adopting from a shelter. It is very rare that you will find Guinea Fowl up for adoption. But, you can check nevertheless. You can even adopt a wild bird and give it a loving home. The last option with adoption is providing foster care for birds. If you want to bring home your friend's birds, make sure that you know everything about the diet and the health requirements of the bird. That way you will not be in for any surprises.

Livestock feed stores order chicks and keets sometimes. This is usually seen in the months of spring. One store that is known for adopting this practice is the Tractor Supply Company. You can check for the breeds that are being brought in. If Guinea Fowl are included in this list, you can collect them when they arrive. The only challenge you will face is guessing the gender of the bird. In addition to that, you may also find it hard to spot Guinea Fowl hatchlings if you are new to them. So, it is a good idea to take an experienced person along.

Lastly, you can even check online or in local advertisements. There are several online options for those who want to bring birds home. Craigslist is one place that you are most likely to find newly hatched birds up for sale. You even get great offers and deals with these listings. Just make sure that you are buying from a genuine seller. So, checking the bird beforehand is recommended when you are ordering them online. If not, you may end up with unhealthy birds, or even birds from an entirely different species altogether.

Guinea Fowl Fact: Some hatcheries or breeders provide the option of 'surprise chick' with every flock of birds that you buy. This means that only one bird will be of a different species. It is better to not opt for this as you cannot be sure of the bird that you will get. If you are unequipped to take care of the bird, you may end up with a bird with several health issues. Worse still, if the bird is not meant to be raised alone, you may have to invest in more birds that you may not even want.

While the options of buying birds are many, you need to make sure that you bring them home at an age that is feasible for you to provide care and support to the bird. It is recommended that you do as much back work and learn more about the bird before you make the commitment. You can either bring home eggs, keets or even adult birds depending upon the facilities that you have in your home. You also need to prepare your home differently for every stage that you bring your bird home in. The next section tells you all about this.

Guinea Fowl facts: Helmeted Guinea Fowl are not as expensive. Normally, a single bird will cost you between $14-$20 or £7-£15. You can even order a clutch of ten hatchable eggs for $100-$120 or £55-£80. Vulturine Guinea Fowl are the most expensive birds costing almost $250-300 or £100-150 per bird.

e. How old should the bird be?
You have three options when choosing the age of the bird or the stage that you want to bring it home in. The three options are:

Eggs

You can bring home eggs and hatch them in your home. If you already have a flock of Guinea Fowl, you will be surprised to know that hens willingly adopt the eggs that you bring in. If not, you will have to invest in incubators that can provide the warmth that the eggs need and help them hatch. We will talk about incubation in more detail in the 'breeding' chapter.

You have several sources to obtain eggs from. Of course, you can hatch the eggs of your own flock. If you have neighbors with Guinea Fowl, you can even ask them for eggs to hatch in your home.

There are several online auctions for Guinea Fowl eggs. You also have online breeders who sell eggs. It is not possible to know about the quality of the eggs that you get from these breeders, however. You can send in your queries and see how they answer them. If they are genuine, they will write back to you soon and will be open to any questions. The best option is a local hatchery or breeder.

Make sure that you do not accept eggs that are too large or too small. They should also be clean when you get them from the breeder. If you are getting them shipped, expect a few of them to be damaged in the process.

Keets

Keets are the hatchlings of Guinea Fowl. This is the best option for a new owner. You can bring home a dozen keets and take good care of them. They are also much easier to train at this age and are also easy to house break.

You need to make sure that you meet the light and temperature requirements of these birds. We will discuss in detail about providing the necessary conditions for the keets to develop properly in your home. When you are able to fulfil these requirements, most of the work is done.

Adults

You should bring home adult Guinea Fowl only if you are looking for immediate pest control on your farm. You can buy adult birds from some breeders. You can even adopt birds if you find them. Remember, adult Guinea Fowl are a handful and you may have a tough time getting them used to your home.

They do not require as much care as the keets or the eggs, on the bright side. All you need to do is make sure that they have enough clean water available. Of course, you need to make feed available to them. When you bring birds home for pest control, you won't have to invest in too much feed either.

If you are getting adult birds home, it is advisable to keep them in an enclosure for at least two weeks so that they get used to their home. The problems with these birds is that they tend to wander a lot. If you leave them out in the garden as soon as they come, there are good chances that they will escape or just disappear in the woods or down the street.

You need to let them out one after the other after the confinement period. When Guinea Fowl are alone, they do not wander much. Let one bird learn his way around your home. Then you can let another bird out. If you notice that the two birds are confined to your home and do not wander away, you can let the others out too.

Chapter 3: Progression of Guinea Fowl

The incubation is a lengthy process. We will discuss it at length in the upcoming chapter. But, how do you take care of keets after they hatch or when you bring home some keets? Watching them progress and ensuring that they achieve some milestones will make sure that they are healthy. You will also know what to do with the birds when they reach a certain stage. In this chapter, we will discuss the progressions that your bird should make based on their age. We will start from day 1 and go on till they are juveniles.

a. Preparing for Keets

Before you bring the keets home, you need to make sure that you are prepared to have them. They need to be kept indoors for at least two weeks with perfect temperature and light conditions. You can either keep them in a cardboard box or a cage. The latter is a better option as the birds tend to jump out of the box after a few days.

You need to obtain a heat lamp that will ensure that the temperature is consistently at 95 degrees Fahrenheit. You must have a thermometer with you to make sure that the temperature remains constant at all times. You need to experiment and fix the height before the keets arrive. If you want to increase temperature, the lamp needs to be lowered. If you want to decrease the temperature, the lamp needs to be lifted up. The temperature will be lowered by 5 degrees when the keets are a week old. This whole set up is called a brooster.

Guinea Fowl facts: The lamp that you need is an Infrared Lamp. You can order them online or can obtain them from most stores that cater to livestock. It is ideal to have a 250 watt lamp. If this set up is hard for you to arrange, you can even purchase readymade broosters online. They are a little expensive but are much easier to use and operate for first time Guinea Fowl keepers.

The next thing you need is some bedding at the bottom of the cage. Avoid any sort of wood shavings or chips as the birds tend to swallow them, ending up with clogged intestines. Instead, you can use paper towels or even newspaper.

Food and water should be available in abundance for the keets. It is good to start off with turkey starter feed for your keets. This feed contains about 20% more protein than the feed available for keets on the market. This feed is also medicated with Amprolium to make sure that the birds do not get coccidiosis. Birds raised on this feed tend to be healthier and larger.

Fresh water is a must for keets to grow well. You can get a water dispenser from the market or a pet store. These contain an inverted bottle that slowly dispenses water out in to a plate. You also have the option of using a mason jar lid for water. But, make sure that you use large marbles to fill the plate with water. The chicks will slowly suck the water out from between the marbles. If you leave the plates as is, the chicks are at a risk of drowning. Feeders are commercially available. It is a better option to invest in these feeders instead of using a plate or the lid of a mason jar. This will make sure that the keets do not walk on the food or spill it.

b. First two weeks

The first two weeks are very crucial to determine the health of your keets. Maintain the temperature at 90 degrees now as it helps them grow. You will still keep the birds on the Turkey starter feed as it is fortified with necessary medication for the birds.

Just to be sure of any temperature fluctuations, you could get a digital thermometer and place it in the cage at all times. This thermometer will be able to record the maximum and minimum temperatures. That way you can even see how the keets respond to any temperature fluctuations within the cage.

Retain the marble water dispenser and the feeder as the chicks are still too small. They will dirty their food and water dispensers if they are open and may even spill the food in them. At this stage, you need to make sure that the feeder and the water dispenser is always full. The keets are growing and will need as much nutrition as possible. You will also see that they are always hungry and will keep on pecking at the food.

If you want your Guinea Fowl to be tame, you need to handle them as much as you can from their younger days. Make sure you carry the chicks on your palm. Just be very careful when you are handling them. You need to pick them up from beneath with your palm cupping gently. Be very careful about their delicate little feet. They should not bend in awkward directions that may lead to breaking or deformities. Keep your hands clean when you are handling the birds. That way there are no infections within the flocks.

Keeping the birds entertained is a good idea. One of the best things for Guinea Fowl is to keep a mirror in the cage. Fix a framed mirror on one wall of the cage. The frame protects the birds. These birds simply love their own reflection and will spend all day looking and pecking at themselves.

You can even hang a few toys into the cage. Watching them peck at the toys, scratch at the bedding and even stare at their own reflection is pretty entertaining! You could just sit there all day and observe the keets that are busy with self-devised games.

c. White Millet Taming

For those of you who are bringing home Guinea Fowl as pets, white millet training is super important. Of course, your keets need to be trained even when you are planning to rear them on your farm because it makes it easier to get them to come to you when called. This training can start from day one. You need to be patient if you have a large flock as the birds respond quite differently to this training.

White millet is easily available at any feed store. You need to make sure that the millet is pure white in color and does not have any red or yellow millet mixed in. This is purely a treat and will not replace the food of your keets. Find some constant cue words such as "come little chicks, "here chick, chick" etc.

You can begin this training right on Day 1 but you will probably get very little response. Hold the millet out in your palm and call out to the birds. On the first day, the keets feed on the yolk and are pretty much full all day. You can try by holding a keet in one hand and placing the millet in the other hand and showing it to the bird. If you have a large flock, this is not practically possible. But if it is just a dozen or so, it is worth the try. You will notice that some of them peck at them and some of them just ignore this training.

On the second day, the millet is of interest to the keets as they are hungrier. But they will be a little hesitant to come to you still. But you need to keep showing the millet to the keets and repeat your phrase. If you are lucky one or two will come to you.

By the third day, the keets will warm up to you and will respond to your call. If they come running to you, you need to hold the palm down to the bottom of the cage so that the keets can peck at it and taste the millet. Once they have relished the white millet, you can be sure that they will come to you again and again. White millet works wonders when it comes to training Guinea Fowl.

However, you need to make sure that they do not get used to the white millet. For a few days you may use this as a treat. Then, when the birds realize that your hands carry treats, they will come running to you even when you keep their regular feed in your hand. They will enjoy eating from your hands and will actually be quite a riot as soon as they see you. Even when you have a feeder in the cage, the birds will want to eat from your hand because in their mind, what is in your hand is tastier and more fun than the boring food in the feeders.

What you need to understand is that all the chicks may not become equally tame. Some are tamer than the others because that is their inherent personality. However, you need to semi tame them at least so that they are able to adapt to a domestic set up. So hold up the millet and call out to all your birds. You need to repeat this at least 3 times each day to make sure that your keets respond properly to your call.

Once they are tame, you can have a blast by placing your palm and getting the keets to come to you and peck at your palm in sheer excitement. They will start walking on your arm and will even come to you when you just approach the cage. This shows that the birds are tame and enjoy the company of human beings. The only thing you need to do is be extremely patient.

d. Moving them to the Coop

When the keets are about 14 days old, you can move them to the coop. However, you can even make this move at 10-12 days if you feel like they are getting too big for the brooster. When that happens, you will notice that the brooster looks a lot more crowded than before and there isn't any space for the birds to move around. They will keep running into the walls. When you see the birds trying to fly, it is a sure shot indication that they are ready for the coop.

There are different types of coops that you can get for your Guinea Fowl. We will talk about them in detail in the following chapters. If you are moving the birds when it is cold outside, you need a heat lamp in the coops as well. It is always recommended

36

that you get birds into your home in the warmer months. That way when you make the move, it is easier on the birds. Even when you move the birds during summer, you need to keep the heat lamp on at night to make sure that they are warm.

On the first night, it is quite normal for them to huddle up to one another as it is a new place and a new setting for them. Keep the food and water bowls close to the lamp on the first night so that they have something familiar around them. Then, you can move it away on the second night.

Unlike other birds, keets are not scared of change. They will take about one hour to get used to their new home and will be quite comfortable. The coop gives them the luxury of foraging and you will see that they start scratching around for bugs as soon as they are a little comfortable.

Do not change the feeders or the water dispensers as the birds are still quite tiny in size. Make sure all the windows and doors have chicken wire around them. The keets are still quite defenceless and will fall prey to predators very easily.

e. Perching

When the birds are about 20 days old, they look much bigger. Their feathers should have started growing by this time. They are advancing towards adult behavior patterns. They will make sounds similar to adult birds. You will notice that the female and the male birds have very distinct calls.

When the birds are 20 days old, one important behavior pattern that you will see is perching. When you have any perching space at a certain height, your birds will go up there at night. Of course, that means that your birds are good flyers now.

Perching is instinctive to Guinea Fowl because they need to keep an eye on what is happening around them. They love playing watchdogs and hence require a place that is at a decent height where they can watch over their own space. So, you need to build perches for your birds in order to help them rest comfortably at night.

If you have a large flock, you need to have a coop that is high enough to provide perches for all the birds. These perches can be at equal or different heights. Based on the pecking order of the birds, they will occupy these perches.

f. At 6 weeks

This is an important milestone for the Guinea Fowl because their feeding habits will change. You will no longer give them the starter feed. Instead, you will start to switch to grower feed. This change needs to happen gradually to make sure that you do not overwhelm the birds. Add a few grower pellets to the feeder. Increase this quantity when the birds are eating the grower feed fondly. You can slowly switch over to the grower pellet completely. You also need to change the diet of the birds slowly to enable them to adjust their digestive system to the new nutrients that are being provided by the new food.

By now, the polka dot-like speckles are clearly visible on their feathers and all their feathers are completely formed. They are able to fly well and have grown to almost their full capacity. You will see that these birds will bicker with one another in order to establish a pecking order within the group. This may become a little aggressive at times, making it necessary for you to intervene. However, Guinea Fowl are known to be a lot gentler than ducks and chickens when it comes to establishing a pecking order.

g. Ready to free range

After 6 weeks, your Guinea Fowl are more than ready to free range because they are as large as adults, almost. They are no longer threatened by farm animals or pets like cats and dogs. They like to stick together as a flock and will only move around together. This is the best time for them to free range as they are at a very low risk of injuries and falling prey to predators. Usually this happens by the time they are 8 weeks old.

By now, the birds know that the coop is their home base. When you want them to free range, you should not take them out. Just leave the door open and wait for them to venture out on their own. The outside world is very new to them and they may or may not jump right at the opportunity of walking out. They will take their time. First, the birds begin by perching on top of the door, trying to take a look at the world around them. When they feel safe they may just step out and walk around a bit. You will notice that one of them is the bravest of the flock. Slowly, the rest of the flock will join the birds one by one.

If you have any other animals on the farm such as cats or dogs, the Guinea Fowl will take time to check them out. They will perch on the door and keep an eye on these new creatures. If they feel safe, they will come down. Some of them may not be so sure of it and may head back into the coop. Don't force them out and let them take their time to move into the outside world on their own.

You can make the first experience of moving out more fun by waiting outside with some white millet. That will make them associate the world outside with positive reinforcement and will feel like they should come out more often. Of course, this is a stressful time for the birds as they are trying to figure out what lies on the other side. If it is you with a hand full of white millet, they will be delighted.

Now, what you need to know about your Guinea Fowl is that they have very poor memory. If you let them out the top door, they will not remember that it is the same way back in. Instead, they will try to walk into the chicken wire on the lower windows or doors. They will relentlessly peck at the wire and head butt it to get in. Give their memory a boost and just pick them up to let them back in. Doing this a couple of times will help them remember how to get back into their own coops. Even if one of the birds in the flock figures out how to get in and out, the rest of them will just copy him and follow suit.

When they are out free ranging after they have learnt to get in and out of the cage, you also need to be aware that they may meet other animals in or around your home. It is not easy to have birds like ducks and chickens in the same space as guineas sometimes. You need to make sure that you have taken all the necessary precautions to ensure that none of your pets get hurt in the process of getting to know one another. The most heart breaking thing is to see one of your guineas or other birds fatally injured in a surprise attack or fight.

Chapter 4: Managing your Guineas

If you only have Guinea Fowl in your home, the dynamics are quite different from having guineas with other poultry birds. If you are keeping guineas on a farm, especially, it is likely that you have other birds like chickens or ducks in the same place. It is alright to have many birds together, but you need to take care of the requirements of each individual species to make sure that they are content and happy. It has often been observed that when you try to just collectively raise the birds with the same feed and the same water dispenser, they will immediately try to establish a pecking order. This means that you will not only have fights within the individual flocks but also between the flocks. To prevent that and make it easier for you to keep your Guinea Fowl with other birds, here are a few things that you can try:

a. Coop management

Diseases spreading between different species of birds is the biggest concern. In fact, some diseases that affect chickens are a lot more serious when they affect Guinea Fowl. So, it is advisable that you keep a check on the cleanliness of the coop irrespective of the types of birds you have on your farm. Whether it is guinea fowl, turkeys, chickens, geese or ducks that you plan to keep together, you need to make sure that the coop is always clean if you are going to house them together. If you have the space, it would be ideal to get each species of bird a coop of their own.

Like any bird, poultry birds also need to be quarantined before you introduce them to a fowl. You need a special quarantining coop for this where the new birds can be housed for 30 days before they are introduced to one another. Now, coming to the cleanliness of the coop, you need to be a lot more cautious if you live in a warmer part of the world. It is quite simple, the warmer the weather, the higher the chances of diseases spreading.

Even if you do have separate coops, a good idea would be to keep the coops very clean because free ranging birds can walk into the coops of other birds. Sometimes, the birds may get along. Other times they may just steal food from one another. When the latter happens, the leader of the flock always shoos out the birds he doesn't want in his coop.

The most important thing with respect to coop cleanliness is keeping it dry. If the coop is dry, it does not smell as much. If you are keeping birds like chickens or ducks with guinea fowl, you have to be extra cautious. The poop of guinea fowl is not as messy as chickens or ducks. So, they do not know to keep away from the poop and may step in it unknowingly.

The litter or the bedding needs to be dry. If it is a good absorbent, you can achieve that easily. When you have water fowl like ducks along with guinea fowl, the litter material needs to be mixed up. This ensures that the webbed feet of these birds do not compress the litter. That way, the absorption reduces. Of course, with Guinea Fowl you also have the advantage of their habit of scratching. So, whenever the litter flattens, they will scratch it right up for you.

b. Make space

It does not matter how many kinds of birds you have in your home or on your farm. The crucial thing is space. All the birds should have enough space to run around, forage and keep themselves entertained. If your birds are bored, they will just peck at each other and fight. It will also become quite a challenge to keep the space free from feathers and poop. If you have enough space for the birds, the pecking order is not as intense as it would be when they are in a confined space. That way, if one of them is being pecked or attacked, they can at least run away and hide. Of course, cleaning becomes convenient for you as the birds will have space to wander and won't come in your way.

Coop training your birds is extremely important. That means your birds need to get into the habit of sleeping in the coop every night. This is certainly not fun as they become very restless, especially when they are kept together. Remember that having more than one type of bird in a coop requires space even inside the coop. When they are being coop trained, the birds are restless and stressed. That means that the chances of catching diseases are a lot higher. That is why you need to keep the space as large as possible.

When you are coop training them, the birds will be extra loud, will poop a lot more, will shed a lot more feathers and if you have birds like ducks around, they will spill all the water in the water bowls of other birds. This is something you need to ignore and keep cleaning the coop. At the end of two weeks, when you let the birds out, you will see that their personality is almost unrecognizable. The birds are so happy to be outside that they will forget about fighting one another or pecking at each other.

Make the coop training period easier on the birds by ensuring that they have enough food and water. That will keep them calm and less anxious. If the space is small, be prepared to clean the coop more often. When the birds are being trained, they also need a lot of roosting space. If they do not have this, they will have nothing to do all day and will get antsy. On the other hand, when they do have the space they need to roost, they will spend all their time there.

For birds that like to scratch, leaving something for them to scratch at during the day is a great idea to keep them entertained. Material like straw with some seeds in them is ideal for birds like Guinea Fowl. While the chickens and guineas scratch this straw, the ducks will forage through it.

c. Managing different birds
You need to have a system in place to make sure that they birds are being fed well, cleaned properly and given enough water to be content. This system depends on what birds you have in the coop really.

Now, the first thing you need to do is keep a good male to female ratio to reduce stress among the birds. If you have chickens, it is good to have seven hens for every rooster. With ducks, 5 females for every drake that you have is a decent ration. With guinea fowl, their monogamous nature will prevent this issue. If there are too many males in the group, they tend to fight and will even be aggressive towards the female birds. Now, for instance, if drakes in your group do not have enough female ducks during the mating season, they may even go after the chickens or guineas and hurt them. You can avoid this by making sure that the male to female ration is good. If you do not want to change the numbers in your flock, you will have to provide the birds with their own individual space or coop.

Watering issues
If you have Guinea Fowl with water fowl like ducks, you need to find a good watering system. You see with water fowl, any open water bath is a chance for them to play and really get dirty. This is not really advisable. So, for these birds, you need to have and auto waterer that will dispense water when needed. If you want to use a bowl, elevate it with a cinder block to make sure that the birds do not climb into them. Ducks tend to spill a lot of water and make the space messy.

You get nipple waterers as well. Do not opt for them as your birds won't be able to drink out of them easily. When that happens, birds tend to get annoyed and will just choose not to drink any water at all. You can provide multiple waterers to ensure that all birds get enough to drink.

Feeding issues
Having one large feeder is the method adopted by most poultry owners. If you have Guinea Fowl, it is best that you do not follow this method because the birds tend to take full control of the feeder. They will peck at any bird that comes anywhere close to the feeder. So, have two large feeders so that even the birds that are lower in the pecking order get to eat. If you don't want to keep two feeders, you can scatter some of the feed on the floor to make sure all the birds can eat enough. A flock that is fed well tends to get along better. You can even let them out to forage after a

feeding session to make sure that they have enough in their bellies. That way they are happier for longer.

When the coop has diverse birds, figuring out what to feed them can be a little difficult. Now, the protein required for different birds is different. Some people get special feed that is prepared with all the requirements of the birds in mind. Now, this is a little expensive as it is custom made. It comes in a pellet form. If you can afford to give your birds that, it is ideal. However, you can also make a mixed bag of foods for your birds to keep them well nourished.

You can buy your regular feed from the stores and mix it up with chick crumbles, laying mash and scratch. Then, if your birds are also free ranging, they can choose the foods that they want. If you want, you can even put some game bird feed on the floor for birds like the Guinea Fowl so that they get the additional protein that they need. People tend to feed birds a lot of scraps, cereal and left overs. This is good too if you are not going to make it a habit. You can take a big bucket of leftovers from time to time and leave it out for the birds to eat.

This way, your birds get to choose what foods that they want to eat. This is also an economical option for most bird owners. Free ranging is also an additional source of nutrition for birds.

Nesting and Roosting issues
This is one of the most important things when you are dealing with a mixed group of birds. You need to give the birds the kind of nest that they need to bring out the nesting instinct in them. Now, if you have large birds like the turkey, it is best that you give them a nest on the floor. This is true even for the water fowl. The nesting box that you use should be at least twice the size of the bird.

Sometimes, they end up laying eggs in each other's nesting box. When you keep any nesting boxes on the floor, make sure that they are in a secluded part of the coop to ensure that the chickens and guineas do not go and scratch them up.

With guineas, the problem is that they will lay eggs everywhere in the beginning. Then, once they are into the second breeding season, they tend to make their own nest boxes. A nest box is not really recommended for guineas as they are not so fond of it. Instead, get a piece of wood that is square shaped. Place it against the wall to make a small triangular space in between. They prefer to lay eggs in this space. Even with water fowl, this technique works but you need to get a really big piece of wood so that they have enough room.

Having high roosts is a must for coops with birds like turkeys and chickens. These birds like to have a roost above the ground level. For turkeys and guineas, this roost needs to be really high and long to make sure that they feel comfortable. The chickens will take up lower roosts. In case you are not able to arrange for high roosts, you need to make sure that you have several roosts that are placed away from one another. That way, they will not kick off.

If you have water fowl, they like to stay close to the ground and will roost in the warmest parts of the coop. They may even sleep near the nesting boxes.

When you have multiple birds, you need to work a lot harder at keeping them content. For instance, just having a pond is not enough for the ducks or just letting them forage around is not good enough for guinea fowl and chicken. They should not feel threatened by one another and should be able to live peacefully.

d. Guinea Fowl and other Pets

If you have dogs or cats in your home, you need to be really careful when the Guinea Fowl are younger, as they do not know how to tackle these large creatures and will end up getting injured. When you have keets in your home, make sure that you keep them out of your dog/ cat's reach. They should be in a secluded room that is far away from the dogs or cats.

When you shift your young birds to the coop, they are still too little to be introduced to the dog or the cat. Make sure that all the doors and windows of the coop are covered with chicken wire.

That way, they are all safe from these larger animals. In the natural order, Guinea Fowl are prey animals. There are many instances when Guinea Fowl are eaten up by dogs of the owner's neighbors or simply killed. Even if your dog is extremely gentle, he is a potential hazard to these birds, merely because of their place in the food cycle. So be a careful when you are introducing them.

Some people would say that they were comfortable introducing keets to their dogs and cats. This is alright when you have one or two of them and are able to monitor the interaction perfectly. However, when you have a dozen keets, you never know which one may accidentally rub shoulders with the dog and end up being mauled. That is the last thing you want in your home.

When the Guinea Fowl are in the protected coop, allow your dog or cat to explore. They may want to sniff around and try to figure out the new creature you have introduced into the family. Allow them to do this as they at least get used to the Guinea Fowl.

After a few days, you will see that your dog or cat is no longer inquisitive. That is when it is safe to bring the birds out and let them free range while you keep the dog or cat in the same space. When you are letting them interact in the open for the first time, you need to keep the bigger animal controlled or leashed. By the time the Guinea Fowl are ready to free range, they are quite large and it is very unlikely that your cat will go after them. The dog, however, needs to be monitored.

Now, Guinea Fowl are always in flocks and will stay close to one another. Before you let the dog or cat and the birds interact freely, you need to make sure that even the Guinea Fowl are alright with the animal in the same space. The next thing to do is to let the dog or cat free and keep the Guinea Fowl in a temporary fence. That way, they are not threatened and they also get used to the movements of your pet dog or cat.

When they are disturbed, Guinea Fowl can make very loud alarm calls. This may startle your pet, leading to an attack. That is why you need to take good care when you are introducing the animals to one another. They should be introduced in a neutral space where neither one is threatened.

You also need to understand that the pet is at risk of injuries. Guinea Fowl are known to keep predators away with their call. Sometimes, they may even attack any animal that threatens them as a flock and injure the animal quite badly with their sharp claws and beaks.

Make sure that your dog or cat is very comfortable around these birds before making any sort of introductions. In most cases, the Guinea Fowl will be able to run away to safety. For additional security, you should avoid pinioning your Guinea Fowl. That gives them a chance to fly away in case things go awfully wrong. You can never control the behavior of animals as they are purely based on instincts. The best you can do is give them a loving home where they both feel equally secure. When you see any instance of aggression, you need to separate the animals immediately.

e. To pinion or not to pinion

Pinioning is an option that people who want to exhibit their Guinea Fowl or want to keep them in a confined space opt for. Now, pinioning has its advantages:

- It makes sure that your Guinea Fowl do not wander too far away.
- When show birds are pinioned, they are easier to handle. They even tend to attract more visitors to these exhibitions as the birds do not just wander around.
- They prevent the birds from walking out into a main street in case you live near one. That way, death by accidents can be avoided to a large extent.

That said, the question that remains is whether pinioning is a cruel act or not. Now if you think that pinioning is just the same as wing clipping, you are quite mistaken. The former is a permanent procedure while the latter only temporarily disables the birds from flying away.

Normally, people opt for wing clipping in the breeding season. This makes sure that the brooding hens stay within the coop and do not wander away and possibly adopt other little Guinea Fowl. Yes this can happen. In this season, it is recommended that the wings are clipped every 10 to 12 days. That way, the wings that do grow back are kept in full control. This is necessary in the warmer months. If you want your bird not to escape over the fencing, you can clip one of the wings. That puts them out of balance and makes sure that they stay close.

If you are planning to have free range birds, especially, clipping in the breeding season is the best option. That way, in the other months when these birds are wandering around, they can escape when attacked by a predator. Guineas instinctively run. But, that does not mean that you remove their ability to fly altogether.

Pinioning is such a process where the bird is rendered flightless forever. This process is used by people who want to rear the birds for eggs, shows or by even those who are into intensive rearing. This procedure is considered cruel most of the times and there are strict laws in certain countries that limit pinioning to only a few kinds of birds.

When you clip the wings you only cut about 1 inch from the primary flight feathers of the bird. In case of pinioning, the procedure is surgical. Basically, the part of the wing from which the primary wings grow is amputated in this procedure. There are metacarpal bones that are called the pinions. These bones are severed. Alternatively, some guinea owners also go for tendenotomy. This process requires a tendon from the wing to be removed. That way, the bird is fully feathered but is not able to fly normally. Both processes are irreversible and can be very dangerous when the birds are free ranging. Even in the case of determining the pecking order, this process can be harmful as the bird that is being attacked will not be able to fly to safety.

Now, in countries like New South Wales, owners are required to look for alternatives. When they have no other option and if they can justify the need for pinioning, they are allowed to do so. In fact, one cannot have chickens pinioned in this country. Guinea Fowl and other birds like pheasants are allowed to be pinioned because they are a little restless and have often injured themselves by flying straight to the roof of the coop when alarmed. These birds tend to spend a lot of time on the ground even when they are not pinioned. That is why it is permitted to carry the procedure forward.

Now, if you have decided to pinion your Guinea Fowl, you need to have this done before they are three days old. This is the ideal age as the bird's wings are still not developed. In addition to that, they have still not found any use for their wings. So, they are used to being flightless right from the beginning. That makes them choose alternative defence mechanisms when they are attacked or disturbed by a predator or a bird that is higher in the pecking order.

This procedure must be carried out by a registered veterinarian. Sometimes, experienced owners are allowed to do this at home under the guidance of their vet. There is no need to use any anaesthesia for this procedure as the birds will not feel any pain even during the amputation surgery. Only when you are getting larger birds like *megapodes* pinioned is anaesthesia compulsory.

If the bird is over 3 years of age, you cannot perform this procedure at home. Your bird should be pinioned by a vet who is properly registered. You also need to ensure that anaesthesia is given to the bird during this process.

In case you opt for tendonotomy, only a certified vet is allowed to perform the surgery. In this case, too, the bird must be given an anaesthesia. Once you have had your bird pinioned, you are required to keep the coop safe. You need to use night shelter and security fencing to keep the birds safe. In case you have a large flock that is of economic value to you, such as meat or egg production, it is also recommended that you hire a keeper to supervise their safety.

The decision of pinioning your bird is left to you entirely. Although it is heavily criticized, if you have to do this for the safety of your birds, then you must go ahead. Of course, when you know that the bird's life could be in danger, you can look for better alternatives. In the end, making sure that your bird is healthy and safe is the priority.

The next chapter talks about Guinea Fowl care which includes the food and the shelter requirements of the birds. There are so many options with respect to housing and feeding that you need to know about every single one of them before you make a choice.

f. Flock behavior of Guinea Fowl

Guinea Fowl or any other flocking birds will have a certain social hierarchy within the group. The strongest male is the leader of the flock in most cases and the others are subordinates to the leader. Now, if you have multiple species of birds in your flock, they may try to establish a pecking order among themselves too. This leads to bloody battles among the birds. The most notorious birds are ducks which can really harm the Guinea Fowl to establish their place in the group.

Now the selection of the alpha male is quite logical and comes with a set of responsibilities towards the flock.

1. Pecking order

A male Guinea Fowl is chosen as the highest ranking member of the group. This bird will lead all the activities of the flock and will even determine the direction that the birds will forage. It is the job of this bird to keep any intruders away from the flock. In case of Guinea Fowl, there is also a second dominant male just below the alpha. This male will take care of the activities of the group when the primary male and his partner leave the flock for breeding.

The highest ranking male is chosen by a series of small fights with the other males. The one that wins all these fights automatically gets to the top of the pecking order. Now, the privileges and responsibilities of this top ranking male include:

- Leading the group while foraging and determining which direction the group will go in.
- Being the first one to breed and court till he holds the dominant position in the group.
- Initiating all the action required to keep intruders out of the flock. This also includes chasing away new Guinea Fowl that are added to the flock. In the wild, a new bird is a threat to the breeding territory and must be removed immediately.

There is one more male below this dominant male. Under the second head, you will have a non-breeding male. Now, these two male birds will stay close to the dominant bird and will show submissive display, especially the non-breeding male.

The females in the group are usually kept in the middle, just below the males and just above the juveniles. Even in the females, there is one top ranking one who is the primary male's mate, a second one below her and a third non breeding female who will partner with the second male and the non-breeding male respectively.

Even when the primary male and female go away for while during the breeding season, their position in the group remains the same. The secondary male and female will precede the activities and will return to their spot once the primary birds return.

The non breeding are meant to be helpers. Guineas indulge in a practice called cooperative brooding. This is when the helpers will take over the responsibilities of the primary female bird. It has been observed that this female is least caring towards the eggs while the primary male will only step in after the chicks arrive. In some cases, the offspring of the alpha couple from a previous breeding season will brood over the eggs in the current breeding season.

The position of the alpha male can only be challenged by a new male in the group. This could be a bird from another flock or even the offspring. When the alpha is challenged, the two birds will indulge in a fight. In Guineas, this fight can either be very mild or can be really bloody and garish depending upon the personality of the birds. If the young male is successful in defeating the primary male, he takes over his place while the former will retire with his mate to the side of the flock while the new bird takes care of all the activities.

2. Dusting

Guinea Fowl rarely take baths in water baths. They indulge in a habit called dusting or dust bathing. This is a part of the preening process of these birds that allows them to keep their plumage intact. The birds will flap around in dust and work it deep into their plumes. This makes sure that the plumes are free from any grease that can lead to matting. The dust that has soaked up all the oil will be discarded to have clean and oil free plumes. Now, this process also allows the birds to get rid of any parasites, mites, lice etc. The feather becomes smoother and remains clean at all times.

The frequency of dusting really depends on the season and the climatic changes. You need not worry about cleaning your Guinea Fowl as they will take care of it themselves. Only if you notice some grime or dirt stuck to their feathers that won't come off even with dusting, you can use a mild soap solution and wipe it out gently. Gentle brushing is permitted if this debris is too stubborn. Make sure you do not pull any feathers out in the process as it could lead to abscesses and infections.

Chapter 5: Raising your Guinea Fowl

a. What to feed them

When they are younger, Guinea Fowl require a lot of protein in their diet. Almost 25% of their diet needs to contain proteins. With this, you can be sure that your bird develops properly and grows to be healthier. In case special Guinea Fowl feed is not available to you, you can even provide the birds with starter food of other poultry species like turkeys. They also need plenty of water to drink. For babies, you need to ensure that the water is at room temperature or even slightly warm. You must never give your keets cold water.

As the birds approach maturity, you need to change their food habits. The first thing you need to do is lower the protein content of the feed. When they are close to two months of age, they will not need more than 18% of proteins. Once they are mature, you can switch to adult guinea foods.

Adult guineas are very low maintenance birds. If they are free range, they will pretty much fend for themselves. These birds require about 15% of proteins in their diet that they will obtain from foraging and eating different types of insects including beetles, ticks and mosquitoes. In addition to this, free range guineas also enjoy worms, caterpillars, weed seeds and grass. Greens are an important part of a Guinea Fowl's diet. They provide the fibre that is necessary to help the food get digested easily. They will make up for this requirement by foraging through several naturally available options like dandelion.

Since your birds are consuming greens, they also need some grit that will help them digest the greens efficiently. One of the best grit options is oyster shell that can be mixed into their feed. They will eat it along with the grains that they consume.

Now, if you do not allow your guinea to free range, you need to make sure that the commercial food you are purchasing is adequate. It should have the necessary protein content. For adult birds, do not purchase any medicated foods unless recommended by a vet.

If you are not able to find the appropriate adult bird food in a store near you, you can even give them standard layer mash that will give them the protein that they need. You need to make sure that food is always available to your birds. If you notice any poop or dirt in the foods, make sure you change it immediately.

While free ranging is a great idea, you need to make sure that your birds do no not wander around too much. You need to train them to stay as close to home as possible when they are feeding. This can be done by keeping their feeders full of grains and pellets. You can even mix in some grains like millet and wheat from time to time in your guinea's food. That will make them want to stay close to their coop in order to obtain food.

Plenty of clean drinking water should be made available to your guineas for the food to be beneficial to their health. Even if you have a pond or a lake nearby where the birds free range, clean drinking water should be made available in the coop. This is also enough motivation to keep the birds close to the coop. You can get large bowls and fill them with water. Since Guinea Fowl will not really knock the water over or try to bathe in it, you do not have to worry about the water getting dirty. In case you are unable to refill the bowl regularly, an automatic water dispenser is recommended. You see, water from the bowls may evaporate and become unavailable to the birds. With a waterer, you do not have to worry about this. You can fill it up once or twice a day and let them drink. When you use an automatic waterer, observe the birds for a few days. If they find it too hard to drink from it, they may just stop consuming water altogether. That is when you need to switch to a regular bowl to ensure that they are drinking plenty of water always.

Can you give them table scraps?

Guinea Fowl love table scraps. In fact, when people raise a pair of birds as indoor pets, they have observed that the birds simply love to eat from their plate. Table scraps also make great treats for the birds when you are training them to stay in the coop etc. Now, there are a few things that we eat that can be hazardous to the bird's health. Here are a few tips on feeding your bird human food.

- Never give your guinea chocolate. It is toxic to almost all species of birds. Birds tend to have seizures and even disorientation when they are given chocolates.
- You must never give your bird any food that contains caffeine. This includes tea and cola drinks.
- Too much table salt leads to excessive water consumption, tremors, neurological excitement, depression and, in worst cases, death.
- Avoid feeding the birds any onions. It is known to be toxic to cats or dogs. However, there is no documentation available on the effects of onions on birds. So it is best that you avoid it altogether.
- Parsley should not be fed to poultry birds as it may lead to photosensitivity.
- Alcohol will kill your birds.
- Certain seeds may be toxic for birds. Apple seeds for example can lead to death. You also should avoid giving your birds the pits of apricots and peaches as it may lead to the production of toxins within the gastrointestinal system of the bird.
- Remember that all milk products should be avoided. Birds cannot digest milk and will fall terribly sick. Since they are not accustomed to milk as keets, all Guinea Fowl are lactose intolerant.
- Avoid foods like rhubarb and spinach as they contain oxalic acid that will bind all the calcium and make it unavailable to the bird.

The good thing about Guinea Fowl is that you do not have to fuss over their food a lot. Since they forage, most of their diet is taken care of themselves. All you need to do is make sure that they have access to clean water and food in their coop.

Guinea Fowl facts: Each adult bird will not need more than ½ cup of feed every day. In addition to that, they get a lot of food with their free range time. Make sure that you do not over feed the birds to prevent any fertility issues. They also develop fatty organs when they are given too much to eat. If you are spending too much on the food, you are feeding them too much. You should not spend more than $3-4 or £1.5-2.5 per bird per day.

b. Types of feeders available

There are various types of feeders that are available on the market. You need to pick one that is sturdy enough to support all your birds. You also need to make sure that food is dispensed at fixed intervals so that all the birds get enough food to eat. If you just place the food in a large dish, the birds that are higher in the pecking order will take over and leave very little for the birds that are in the lower ranks. Here are some of the best feeder options available to you:

Treadle feeders

These feeders are the best to make sure that the food remains free from dirt and pests. The feeder comes with a small pedal that opens the lid when the bird steps on it. Don't worry about your birds, they are smart enough to figure out how to get their food. This treadle feeder will keep the food safe from rodents that would otherwise steal it.

Plastic feeders

Poultry feeders made from plastic are commonly used by people who rear chickens. This works quite well with Guinea Fowl too. The feeder is cone shaped and is made entirely from plastic. They have a handle that lets you hang it up. A plastic tray is attached to the bottom. Once you load the food from the top, it is slowly dispensed to the tray beneath. This is where your birds feed from. As the tray empties, more food is dispensed.

Troughs

These are the most common type of feeders that you will find in farms and backyards. They are large rectangular boxes that you can fill up with the feed. Then, the birds can just reach and eat the food up when they want to. The disadvantage with this sort of feeder is that it is prone to getting dirty and of course, the rodents have easy access. It may also infest the coop or your barn with rodents.

Grit Hoppers

These are metallic boxes that have a door on them. This door is slightly sloping and can be swung open just like a regular door. When the birds want to eat, they just push the door open and get it. These are smaller feeders, however and are only suitable for a few Guinea Fowl. If you are housing a pair indoors, this is the perfect type of feeder for you.

In addition to that, you also have the option of building feeders at home. People make bird feeders with PVC pipes that are cut in half vertically. They are then drilled with a few holes to make sure that rain water drains out when required. Some people will also use fish feeders for their guineas.

How to choose a good feeder?

Most people with birds like Guinea Fowl will opt for plastic feeders. These feeders can be really expensive and will not even last so long. With your guineas pecking at it, they tend to get damaged really fast. In addition to that, they are not even that sturdy. If the feeder has very little food left in it and there is a strong breeze, it will just topple, causing a lot of wastage.

Nowadays, most commercially available feeders and drinkers are made from galvanized steel. It is recommended that you opt for the same too. There are several advantages of choosing this material:

- The feeder is strong and does not topple easily. Thus, the food remains protected.
- The material is really smooth. That makes it safe for the birds and also makes sure that you are able to clean it up very easily.
- Steel is robust and will not get damaged very easily.

These steel feeders may seem a lot more expensive than the plastic ones. However, they last longer and are available in several sizes and designs that you can choose from. If you are a hobby breeder and have just a few guineas at home, a plastic one might be alright. However, an investment in a good steel feeder is always worth it. You can buy these feeders online or from any local pet supply store. You should be able to find more options online, however.

When you buy feeders, you also need to invest in appropriate accessories to keep the food safe. You need to get a rain shield to make sure that there is no wastage due to rains. These shields can be placed over the feeders. They are simple hoods that you can just fix on top of your feeder.

You may need a trough or an anti-waste grid. When these birds eat in flocks, they tend to be messy. They also throw a lot of food on the ground, leading to severe wastage. If you have a trough or a grid at the bottom of your feeder, you can make sure that the food is kept off the ground easily.

All in all, when you are choosing a feeder, you need to find one that is convenient for your birds to eat from. It also should prevent unnecessary wastage of food. It is a good idea to change the feed every morning. That can be done if you can slowly increase the food quantity to see how much your birds actually consume in a day. Then, very little is wasted and you are able to feed them fresh food everyday too.

c. Housing a Guinea

Guinea Fowl are rather hardy birds that do not need very expensive housing or coops. The only thing that these birds need is enough space to wander around and stay free from any sort of stress. For housing, one Guinea Fowl ideally needs about 3 sq.ft. or a minimum of 2 sq.ft. So you may calculate the total space that is required by your flock.

If you have trees around your home, the Guineas will happily roost in these trees when they are growing. However, shelter is required by the birds since you need to protect them after nightfall, make sure that they are away from the sun, blizzards and other drastic weather changes. You can either build a coop specifically for your guineas or allot a certain room in your barn for these birds.

Now, if you are looking at confining the birds for egg or meat production, space is very necessary. If they have more room, they will be less stressed. The floor should also have a good absorbent material that can stay dry for a few days.

While wood shavings are recommended, I would personally opt for straw as it makes for great scratching material as well. The entire floor should be covered with this material and you must work towards keeping it dry. That means you have to change it frequently. If you only have Guinea Fowl in the coop, the litter will last for several months as these birds are not so messy.

One thing that Guinea Fowl love to do is roost. So, you have to provide perches in the coop. The higher the perch, the better it is. As we discussed before, these birds will happily roost in the tallest tree. So a perch that is high works really well at keeping the bird content.

Heat is another thing that your guineas will require at all times. This means that you need to either insulate the coop effectively or have to provide some artificial source of heat. The latter is a better option as it prevents retention of moisture inside the coop. When there is too much moisture in the coop, the birds tend to develop several respiratory problems. It can also lead to growth of fungi that are harmful for your birds.

If you have pets in your home or if you want the birds to be confined, it is recommended that you keep the birds in a pen that is covered. That way the birds can run around and can even fly peacefully without you having to worry about birds that have escaped. Make sure you do not underestimate the flying capacity of these birds. They can go as high as 500 ft. and can even fly long distances when needed. You also need to remember that these birds can run fast. They will even escape by running or walking away if you are not cautious enough.

In case you have a mixed coop, keeping male guineas with roosters or other male birds all day long is not a good idea. The guinea will end up chasing the rooster around and stressing him out. It is better if you keep them free ranging during the day and only put them in the same shelter at night. You can even put your Guinea Fowl and roosters in the same coop during emergencies like a blizzard. This is when the birds are very alert about the changes in the weather and will bother each other less.

In case you want to encourage egg laying among guineas, you need to provide them with enough nesting boxes. Some people tend to use the same nesting box for hens and Guinea Fowl. In that case, you need to make sure that the guinea hen is in the coop until noon. That way, the chickens will not lay eggs outside in hidden nests of their own.

In case you want to raise guineas for eggs only, you need to give them a coop that will also allow you to enter and exit the area easily. That way, you can collect the eggs that have been laid quite easily. Of course, for free ranging birds like the Guinea Fowl, you also need to provide the coop with some outdoor access. There are coops with a door that opens to let the Guinea Fowl out. Then, they can walk out into a fenced area where they can forage freely.

You can choose from a variety of coop designs. If you have fewer birds, a small coop will do while those who have more birds will need a large coop. There are also portable or immovable coops depending upon the purpose that you are raising Guinea Fowl for. It is good to have a simple wooden coop that you can add several comfort elements into.

Of course, ventilation is very important. You can have high windows or even a few doors on the coop. But, they should be meshed to keep any predator out. Some windows are removable to clean the coop thoroughly.

Any coop that you would use for poultry birds like chickens will work for Guinea Fowl. What you need to ensure is that the birds have enough space. If you do not want to buy a coop, you can even choose to build one yourself. That gives you the liberty to get really creative and make the coops look really pretty. You can add elements that you like, including a light that you can use at night. Building a coop is quite easy and has been explained in full detail in the next chapter.

1. Various Types of Guinea Housing
There are various kinds of coops that you can choose from. Some people would even be open to keeping Guinea Fowl indoors. Here are a few different housing options and the advantages or disadvantages of each type:

The Ark Coop

If you have a home that is prone to predators, making it hard for your Guinea Fowl to free range during the day, the ark coop is the perfect option for them. Sometimes, complaining neighbors may also require you to find alternatives to having your birds free range during the day.

The ark is a great option as it lets your bird get a lot of sunlight while keeping it close to your home. These coops are movable and you can shift them to any part of your house depending upon where you want the bird to free range. You can keep them in a well shaded area if it is too hot. Of course, you can also clean these coops quite easily as they are smaller. Ark coops are easily available in feed stores or farm supply stores. You can even build these coops very easily.

The only disadvantage with these type of coops is that you cannot have more than 10 birds inside.

Traditional chicken house

This is a regular chicken coop that you will see on most farms. It can be used to house Guinea Fowl as well. These coops are known to be extremely sturdy and will stand the test of time.

The best feature of this type of housing is a fenced run that keeps the chickens protected when they are free ranging. This is another good option if you have the issue of predators in your home.

These coops come with all the accessories needed for your Guinea Fowl. There are several roosts on the walls. You will also have nesting boxes. The retractable windows make it easy for you to control the warmth inside the coop. There is a small door that leads to the run. So, the birds do not have to wait for you to let them out.

These chicken houses can accommodate a large flock of Guinea Fowl. Of course, they are not movable because of the size. But, they are long lasting and extremely sturdy.

Poultry shed

These housing options are affordable and simple. You can even build them yourself quite easily. If you want your shed to be portable, all you need to do is build some skids on the base. That lets you shift it around.

Some people like to build these coops on a raised peer to give the birds additional protection from rodents, snakes and other kinds of ground predators. You can even prevent any damage to the floor of the shed due to rains.

The windows of these sheds are usually made of fiberglass that can be used to provide additional ventilation in the warmer months. When you are buying a poultry shed, it is a good idea to look for those with windows that have a sash that allows you to open and close the window. In addition to that, your coop also looks quite furnished.

d. Building a coop

If you have any interest in carpentry and building things from scratch, you will simply love the idea of building a coop for your beloved birds. This not only lets you get creative with the final output but also ensures that you do not spend too heavily on the housing needs of your birds. The material required are quite basic. Here is a checklist for you to start off with:

- Concrete cinder blocks- 8
- Door hinges
- 2X6 treated lumber
- Roof felt paper
- 2X4 treated lumber
- Roof shingles
- ¾ inch plywood sheet
- A level
- 1.2 inch plywood sheet
- Hammer
- Nails (Galvanized ones)
- 2 and 4 inch deck screws
- Hammer
- Table saw
- Jigsaw

You can look on the Internet to find different shapes and designs of coops. The one that you will find instructions for in this chapter is a basic rectangular coop. Remember that you need to allow about 3 sq. ft. for every bird in your coop.

Find a suitable location for the coop. Any place with better water run off is preferred. That way, when you clean the coop you will not have to worry about issues like water logging that can damage the coop severely.

To begin with, level the land in the construction site that you have chosen. That means you need to get rid of any logs, rocks or stones in the area so that your coop has an even flooring. Mark the corners of the house by stacking two concrete blocks in each of the corners. This also determines the floor space of your coop.

Take the 2X6 lumer to make the floor joists. This needs to run every 16 inches on the middle of the floor. Attach these pieces using the nails. The ¾ inch ply will be used to make the actual floor of the coop. You can cut this out with the exact measurements of the floor area. Then place this perpendicular to the joists that you just made.

You now have the base structure that you can build the rest of your coop on. Start by making a frame for the walls. This can be done with square pieces of 2X4 lumber that measure about 32 inches from the centre. Use this to make the side walls and the back wall of the coop. Use the galvanized nails to hold them in place. This becomes the basic frame for your coop.

The front wall is also made in a similar fashion using the 2X4 lumber. However, you need to make sure that you add a door on the front wall. Not only will this let your guineas in and out, but will also make sure that you have access to the coop whenever needed. That way you can clean it up thoroughly. Hold the front wall in place with the nails.

Now, the door that you cut out needs to be fixed on the front wall. This can be done using the 4 inch screws. That will keep the frame and the door intact. Then, when you want to secure the door, use the door hinges to allow easy access to the coop. Cover the door with ½ inch ply to make it sturdy enough to keep the birds protected whenever you are away.

You still have the ½ inch plywood. Use this to cut out sheets that are the exact size of the walls of the frame that you built. Once you have them in place, hold them up against the outside of the wall. Then, hold them in place using the 2 inch deck screw.

If you have a separate foraging area for your guineas, you can even make a separate door for them. A small rectangle of about 12 inches in height and 18 inches in width can be cut from the floor of the coop towards the roof. Don't cut the 2X4 inch frame. Just cut the plywood over the wall.

It is best that you choose a lean to roof. That will keep rain away from the coop and will also look aesthetic in your garden or farm. The roof must slope very slightly and the slope must be directed towards the back of the coop. You can use the 2X4 inch lumber to make this roof. They become the rafters while the ¾ inch ply becomes the sheathing. The roof felting needs to be attached to this frame as per the instructions provided by the manufacturer. You also need to apply the shingles to finish the coop off.

Now you are ready to add the final touches to your coop. You need to make a ramp at the entrance of the Guinea Fowl door. This should at least be 1 foot above the ground. This makes it easy to direct the birds in and out of the coop.

You need to add some wooden perches too. They should be at least 4 feet off the ground. That makes a secure roosting spot for the birds. They are high enough to watch over the activities that are happening. It is also fulfilling to their instincts as birds that roost.

It is necessary to add an overhead light. This makes it easy for you to access the Guinea Fowl even after sunset. If that is not a feasible option, you can even make use of battery powered torches for the same.

Your coop is now ready. Add the necessary absorbent material to make sure that your bird's feet stay protected. Lastly, you need to cover all the doors and windows with mesh. That certainly keeps the predators at bay and ensures that your birds are able to have a peaceful time every night.

Of course, you have the liberty to paint the coop as you like. Just make sure that you use odorless paints or organic paints to ensure that your birds do not develop any infections or allergies because of the chemicals in the paint. You can even add some toys to make the coop more interesting.

e. Keeping the coop clean

When you have any pet, you need to make sure that you maintain high standards of hygiene. This allows the animals to stay clear of any infections or diseases. In the case of birds, you need to be extra careful because they are prone to diseases. Since you are raising a flock, you also need to understand that the infection or disease can affect the entire flock. If you are raising them for eggs or meat, this implies huge financial losses. In any case, it is hard to take care of a dozen unwell birds.

It is easier, however, to keep their surroundings clean. Keeping the coop clean is of utmost importance because the birds spend the majority of their time there. And, as you know, birds tend to poop and make a mess.

The good news with Guinea Fowl is that they do not make as much of a mess as chickens or ducks unless they are unwell. Even their poop is relatively dry and easy to clean out. Free ranging birds like guineas also tend to dirty their coop a lot lesser as they usually only return to roost and rest in the coop.

That said, you still need to ensure that the coop is clean. If not it can give out a really foul odor in the long run. If you are introducing new birds to the coop, you need to do a thorough round of cleaning. Of course, you need to make a routine that you can stick to for your coop cleaning activities. It is recommended that you disinfect and clean the coop fully at least once every month. Some people only do it once or twice a year. You need to keep it more regular for the benefit of the birds.

Many people will suggest that you use bleaching powder to clean a coop and disinfect it. But the truth is that the fumes left behind by bleaching powder consists of a lot of chemicals that can be harmful for your birds.

Not just that, they can also damage the quality of the eggs and meat if used too frequently. In any case, bleach is a very strong chemical and it is best that you avoid it altogether. Instead, you can choose vinegar as the substitute. The mild acidic property of vinegar gets rid of all the germs and microbes in an organic and safe fashion.

You have the option of using plain vinegar to disinfect the coops. However, if you like it fancy and fresh, make an infusion by soaking orange peels in white vinegar. Add a drop of lemon essential oil to this and leave it for a few days. Then, you can put this mixture into a spray bottle and spray it around the coop for best results. It leaves it fresh and clean for longer. You will also avoid the acidic smell that is quite common with vinegar.

Now, here are a few steps that you need to follow when you clean a coop:

- To start with, let the guineas out or keep them in a temporary fence.
- Then scrape out all the dirt from the coop. This includes the feathers that are stuck to the bottom, the straw or shavings, dirt, manure and any feathers. It is recommended that you shave out guinea manure separately and use it in your farm or garden.
- Once this is done, hose it down fully. That way any solidified grime that is still on the floor will be taken care of. You can even scrub the floor and the walls down if necessary.
- Then you will repeat the process of scraping again. This time all the hardened dirt that has been hosed down will come out too. You will have a fully cleaned floor.
- To add some final touches, you can even sweep the floor of the coop one last time to remove excess water from the corners. Then, you need to let all the water drain out from the coop. If you see small puddles that refuse to drain out, you will have to sweep it out. There should be no moisture in the coop when you are done.

- We now come to the disinfecting part which is of primary importance. In a bucket, mix equal parts of water and vinegar. If you want a deep cleanse, you can even add the vinegar on the floor directly. Now scrub the floor vigorously, ensuring that you get the vinegar all over the coop.

- Then you will rinse the coop out finally and sweep the extra water out just like you did in the first time. Now your coop is almost dry and fully clean.

- The next step is to open all the doors and windows of the coop and allow it to air dry. Allowing the coop to be exposed to the sun also helps a great deal in disinfecting it. Of course, letting in some fresh air will work really well for your coop and will get rid of any unpleasant smells, if that is an issue you are facing.

- Make sure you wash the food trays, the waterers and also the roosts. Making removable roosts will make it easier for you to clean up the coop thoroughly. You need to wash all these coop accessories with the vinegar solution to make sure that they are fully disinfected.

- Lastly, when your coop is dry, lay out fresh bedding material. You can even spray on some orange infused vinegar to make the coop clean and fresh.

To make the process of cleaning easier, it is a good idea to rotate the litter frequently. This is especially true if your Guinea Fowl are sharing their coop with other birds. Of course, you can clean more regularly to make it easier on yourself to clean the coop. With Guinea Fowl, you will have little problem with pests like flies and ticks as the birds will clean this up themselves quite efficiently.

f. Managing predators

If you have poultry birds, you need to expect predators. There are several predators that are lurking around your home that can cause harm to your Guinea Fowl. Most people will have Guinea Fowl on their farm to protect chickens. This is because Guinea Fowl make excellent watch dogs. When they see or hear a predator, they will be able to alert you with their loud and incessant calling.

But, sometimes, when your guineas are alarmed by just about anything, you may feel like they are crying wolf even when a real predator comes. This leads to a lot of owners neglecting the call of their Guinea Fowl.

While they are birds that attack in flocks and pretty much stay in a flock, they can be quite defenceless against predators. You need to take as much precaution as you can besides just providing the birds with shelter at nightfall. The first thing you need to do is identify whether you have a predator problem or not.

1. The different predators out there
There are various predators that will attack your guinea. Some may attack for food while others may attack for sport. Some of the most common Guinea Fowl predators are:

Coyotes and dogs
Pet dogs are unlikely to attack the birds. However, if you have more than one dog at home or if your neighbor has more than one dog, there could be some unfortunate incidents. You see, then the dogs may display pack instincts. There are several factors that turn a dog into a predator. One of them is the breed of the dog and another important factor is the past experiences of the dog with birds or the guineas. There are several instances when dogs that have been successful in obtaining food after attacking the coop have repeated the same behavior. Now, there are several breeds like the sheepdog that will actually protect your birds.

In case of coyotes, they tend to travel in large groups but will attack only in pairs. These creatures are nocturnal and will mostly attack at night. However, there are times when they have attacked even during the day. In fact, coyotes are known to have been diurnal. Because of habitat pressure caused by human beings, they have switched their habits.

Bobcats
These are the most common predators in America. They are two times the size of an average pet cat. They can only attack when the light is low because that is when their eyesight is at its best.

That means that they are most likely to attack at dusk or dawn. These predators have the ability to carry off one full grown adult guinea easily. They may eat the whole bird in one sitting and when they are unable to do so, they will carry the carcass with them. They are usually found in woodlands. If you live in an area that is close to one or encroaches one, you are likely to encounter this predator.

Sometimes, even the domestic cat can become a predator to guineas. They are very messy when they eat and will leave parts of the bird around even after they are done eating. They will eat up all the meaty portions and leave the skin of the bird behind. They also leave marks of their teeth on the bones that they leave behind. Even well fed domestic cats are potential predators.

Foxes
Red foxes are a major threat to poultry. They will attack the bird and catch it by the throat to kill it. They will also bite the bird on the back and the neck to ensure that it is dead. If a fox has been in your guinea's coop, you will see that there are several drops of blood and feathers strewn around. The thing with foxes is that they will also eat up the eggs of the bird. When they eat eggs, they will only eat the insides of the egg and leave the shell behind. As for the bird, they will carry it away with them after they have killed it. If you live close to open plains or woods, you are likely to have attacks by foxes.

There is another type of fox called the grey fox that is the only type to climb trees. These predators will occupy hollow cavities that you can find in old trees.

Raccoons
These are the most notorious predators. They can enter the coop and kill several birds in one attack. They will just open the breast up by chewing and tearing and will eat all the entrails. If they have access to the eggs, they will carry them away from the nest and eat them. If you have several garbage cans outside your home, you are sure to attract raccoons. If they are settled in a certain

area, they are really hard to get rid of. They will look for all the food options available including your precious guineas.

Weasels

Weasels are the smallest and sneakiest of all predators. They are not very common and are trapped very rarely. These creatures have long and slender bodies that they will wrap around their prey. Then with a sharp bite just below the skull, they will kill the bird. They can get into a coop from a hole that is just about 1/4th of an inch in diameter. They can even get through chicken wire, actually. They eat a lot and need to get up to 4 times their body weight's worth of food in a day.

Skunks

Skunks may not really harm your flock. They are more interested in the eggs. They will open the shell up just enough to get access to the contents and lick it all out. If they ever attack a flock, they may only kill one or two birds and will end up mauling the rest of them. These animals do not carry the eggs with them but will eat it right there giving owners the impression that the egg has actually hatched!

Opossums

Opossums are quite similar to skunks. When they attack, they may not kill many birds but will certainly maul a lot of them. They prefer the eggs too. However, when they eat the eggs, it is mashed up and very messy. They even chew the shell and spit it out in the nest. They will rarely attack adult birds and will most often go for the younger ones.

Snakes

Guinea Fowl are known to be very aggressive towards snakes. They will kill a snake in most cases. However, there are chances that the snake gets a hold of the younger defenceless guineas. If a snake is your predator, it is very hard to identify as they leave no traces behind. Snakes will most often go after the eggs of your guinea and just swallow it up as a whole. One interesting thing about snakes is that they will attack your birds or eggs only if the entrance hole of the coop is large enough to let the snake out even after it has eaten. If not, they may enter but will cause no harm to the birds.

Hawks

There are various types of hawks that can hunt your Guinea Fowl down. The most common type of hawk is the red tailed hawk. These hawks attack from hunting areas that are open. They also need to have several perches that they can use to examine the area of attack. Red shouldered hawks that are mostly known for preying on chicken can also be a potential threat to Guinea Fowl. They are also known as hen hawks.

Owl

Not all types of owls will hunt Guinea Fowl down. They normally eat rodents and smaller animals. The one type of owl that may attack your Guinea Fowl is the great horned owl. Other owls like barn owls may only scare your Guinea Fowl with their deafening screeches but will not really attack. Owls are common predators in grasslands, open fields and even woods. They will normally attack at night and take your bird at night. They can even hunt down birds like ducks that are much larger than them in size.

Now, the next challenge that you will face is identifying which predator is hunting your birds down. If you notice that your adult birds are suddenly missing or that the size of your flock is diminishing, you need to become alert for predator activity. Understanding which predator is attacking your flock may be the first step towards solving the problem immediately. They will normally attack at night. They can even hunt down birds like ducks that are much larger than them in size.

Now, the next challenge that you will face is identifying which predator is hunting your birds down. If you notice that your adult birds are suddenly missing or that the size of your flock is diminishing, you need to become alert for predator activity. Understanding which predator is attacking your flock may be the first step towards solving the problem immediately.

2. Which predator is on the loose?

Each predatory animal has its own behavior pattern. They will leave behind some obvious clues that help you decide which animal is actually attacking your flock. Here are a few tell all signs of different predators in your area:

- If you notice that your adult birds are missing but there is not sign of any other damage or disturbance, the most likely predators are hawks, owls, bobcats, coyotes, foxes or dogs. Since these animals kill and carry their prey away, the will normally not leave any signs. As we discussed in the previous section, some of them are nocturnal and some diurnal. Depending upon when your birds go missing you can narrow down the options more.

- If you notice that the chicks are missing and there is no other disturbance, then the culprit is a house cat, raccoon or snake. These predators will leave wings and feathers scattered around at a small distance from the coop because they are unable to swallow all these parts of the bird.

- In case you notice that your Guinea Fowl are dead but have not been eaten, then the culprit is most likely a weasel. These animals usually kill for fun. The insides of your bird may be eaten up in some cases. If the other Guinea Fowl are attacked and severely injured, it is most certainly a weasel.

- If you notice headless carcasses of your bird in the coop, then the predator is mostly a raccoon, owl or hawk. These predators may try to pull the bird out through the mesh and then only eat the head, leaving the body behind.

- If you see that the birds are not dead but severely wounded, it could be the work of several predators. If there are bites all over the body, it is the work of a dog or coyote. If the bites are mostly on the chest, it is most likely an opossum. If the bites or on the hocks, there are chances that rats have attacked the flock. Any bite near the cloaca is an indication of weasel predation.

Besides the condition or the bird or the carcass, the next best way to identify the predator is to check the paw marks of the animal.

74

You can look online for normal paw marks of predators. Then match it to the ones near the coop of your guineas. Once you have had a predator attack, spread some talc or sand in the coop. This will make the paw marks clearer and you will be able to identify it easily.

3. Managing predators

Once you are sure that your flock is being attacked by predators, you can take a couple of actions to make sure that any further damage is prevented. As the owner of the flock, you need to first identify the predator. If you are unable to do so yourself, you can look for several experts online who will be able to help you out with this process.

Here are some simple steps that you can take to manage predators in your area:

Look for better fencing options

Guinea Fowl are free ranging birds. That means that they are going to attract several ground predators. Now, with these predators, the best precaution you can take is building movable fences around your area. You can choose electric or non-electric fences. If you are using an electric fence, make sure that the power is only enough to stun the animal but not kill it. This is also safer for your family and other pets in your home. Also, a stunned predator will resist attacking while a dead predator will simply be replaced after a while.

Now, free range birds are not just threatened by ground predators but aerial predators as well. You need to take enough care to make sure that these predators do not get the habitat that they need to plan an attack. Clear out the perch site within 9 meters of your farm or home. This includes isolated trees or any high perching site. Always house your poultry indoors at night. If you need to train your birds to get into the coop at night, you may change the feeding time from dawn to dusk. Choose dusk to refill the feeders for your birds.

You can even provide your birds with a sheltered run. Using orange net overhead is a good idea as birds like hawks can see this color quite clearly. You cannot kill or trap any birds not just for ethical reasons but also because most of these creatures are federally protected.

You can even get temporary pens that serve as great enclosures for your birds when they are free ranging. You can even move it around to give your birds a wider range to explore. At night, always double check the lock of the coop. Do not leave scraps or garbage around the coops as it will attract predators. If there are any birds that are dying or unwell, remove them immediately from the coop.

Some people may advise you to use lighting around the coop to keep predators at bay. This is not the best idea because it can affect the breeding and egg laying cycle of your flock. Periodic noises are also ineffective although many poultry owners will swear by it. Eventually, the predator gets used to these sounds and will attack the flock anyway.

If nothing works you can also contact the federal wildlife services in your state. They will be able to prevent most of the predators in the most ethical manner. You will normally have a state agency that can do this for you. If not, you can even call the US department of Agriculture or any corresponding organization in your country.

g. Transporting Guinea Fowl

In case you decided to breed Guinea Fowl or have to transport them because you are moving or sending a bird to a friend, you need to find a way to do it that is least stressful for the bird. Transporting a bird should be humane and should make sure that the health of the bird is not compromised along the way. There are a few pointers that will help you when transporting the bird:

- If you are transporting the bird by flight, make sure that you choose an airline that guarantees to treat the bird humanely.

Even if they charge a small fee for feeding the bird, you need to bear the expenses.

- Whether you are transporting him by flight or even in your own personal vehicle, the cage that you choose must be appropriate. It should provide the bird with ample ventilation, space and shade.
- You need to ensure that the bird is not injured along the way. This requires harnesses and soft bedding in the cage.
- Make sure you have the bird checked by a vet who deems him fit enough to be transported. If not, he may catch several infections along the way.

Choosing a good container
You can buy special transport container for your guinea. The bird should be able to sit in the cage and should also be able to spread his wings. The bedding should be placed in such a way that the bird is able to balance himself while sitting or standing. The hotter the weather, the more space your bird needs. This is a rule that you will have to keep in mind whilst transporting your guinea. Of course, the container should be sturdy enough to protect the bird in case of any bumps in the journey.

Humane transportation tips
Whether you are having the bird transported to you by a breeder or whether you are transporting Guinea Fowl yourself, you need to make sure that the transportation conditions are humane. Ask the breeder how he will transport the bird to you. Here are some things you should NEVER do when transporting Guinea Fowl or any other bird:

- Transport them in bags, keeping the legs tied.
- In case the bird is not going to be transported immediately or when you are waiting for a transit, you need to keep them in an area that is cool and calm, not in a stuffy box.
- Any bird that is 3 days old or older must never be deprived of water for more than 1 day when they are being transported.
- Never place the cage in the boot of the car. You must also never leave a cage in the car when it is too hot outside.

There are certain laws about poultry transportation that ensure that the birds are treated well. In Australia, for instance, The Animal Care and Protection Act, lays down a couple of rules and guidelines for responsible transport. Any breach of these guidelines can lead to a fee of close to $35,000 or even a whole year in jail. Make sure you check with the federal department in your state to understand the exact guidelines for transporting birds if you do not want to get into too much trouble.

Chapter 6: Breeding and Incubation

This is of great relevance to most Guinea Fowl or poultry owners. Eventually, you will have to understand the dynamics of breeding the bird and taking care of the abandoned eggs if any. Now, Guinea Fowl are seasonal egg layers unlike chickens. So, it is relatively easier to prepare for their breeding season and make sure that they get everything that they need in order to stay healthy and lay good quality eggs.

a. Sexing the Guinea Fowl

The first step towards breeding Guinea Fowl is to be able to distinguish between male and female birds. Since the tow genders look so strikingly similar, this can become quite a challenge. The call of the bird after they have reached 2 months of age is the first distinguisher between the two genders.

Normally, the male guineas have a single syllable sound. On the other hand, the females will have a two syllable sound that almost sounds like 'put-rock' or 'buck-wheat'. Only when the female is excited will she opt for a single syllable call. However, at no point will a male have a two syllable call.

The wattle is much larger in the male birds in comparison to the females. They also have a deeper curve in the wattle. The edges of the wattles are thicker in comparison to the females. By the time they are about 16 weeks old, the wattles of the females may thicken but not as much as the male.

In case of the Helmeted Guinea Fowl, the helmet of the male is larger. The head and the wattles are also coarser in the males in comparison to the females. The difference in these physical features is very minute and will require a little bit of experience to identify and understand.

Now, Guinea Fowl are monogamous. This means that they will only have one partner for their whole life. They will breed with the same partner every season. The partners are picked based on the pecking order. For example, the primary male will pick the female who is on top of the order among the females.

Guinea Fowl are seldom known to display any violent breeding behaviors like ducks. Since their mates are fixed based on the pecking order, they will not try to snatch away one another's partner. Now, when the primary male of the pecking order is defeated by another male, the dynamics are quite simple. Both the female and the male will retire from the alpha post and will move out to the periphery of the flock where they continue to breed with one another in the following breeding season. The pecking order may change with every breeding season if the new birds challenge the authority of the alpha.

Even then, it is not necessary that you mate your birds in pairs. While that is ideal, you need to keep a proper mating ratio for the fertility of the group to be high. If there are too many females per male, the fertility rate comes down. It is ideal to have a 4:5 ratio of males to females.

As per the United States Department of Agriculture guidelines, when Guinea Fowl are confined very closely, it is possible to mate 6-8 females with one male. That is when the hens may even share the same nest. Every breeder is used for about 3 seasons.

But the mating ratio, when maintained, leads to optimum fertility of the flock.

b. Managing breeding flocks

The egg laying season normally begins in spring. This is when there is more sunlight. After that, the birds may lay eggs for about 6 to 9 months. If you provide artificial lighting, it is possible for you to extend the laying period by encouraging early laying in the females.

Normally, Guinea Fowl are allowed to free range. However, some owners prefer to confine these birds when the laying period begins. Special houses are created with running porches that have a wired flooring. If your bird is not pinioned, it is not possible to confine it to the yard or the garden. In the wild, guineas normally mate in pairs. If your male to female ratio is the same in your flock, you will notice this tendency in domesticated birds as well.

In many countries, artificial insemination is practiced. The male and the females are kept in separate cages. The volume of semen is very low in Guinea Fowl. Therefore, cross breeding between the domestic roosters and wild hens is a common practice. When they are crossbred, the offspring will grow up to be as large as the domestic bird.

However, the gamey flavor is retained. This is done mostly when people rear Guinea Fowl for meat. Depending upon the strain of the rooster that you are using, hatchability will vary. The offspring that result from this type of cross breeding is called a "Guin-hen". These birds look almost like turkeys when they grow to their full size.

You need to provide the breeders with special food that can cater to their protein requirements. This ensures better hatchability in the eggs that are produced. You will be able to obtain special breeder mash. This contains between 22-24% protein. You need to start with this type of feed a month before the laying season begins. You can even use turkey or chicken mash to get the desired results.

This food should be given to the birds irrespective of whether they are free range or confined. The manufacturer's feeding guidelines should be followed correctly to make sure that the food you are providing is beneficial to the birds. In case your vet recommends any supplements, you may use that as well. A lot of clean water should be available to drink.

c. Production of eggs

The breeding and management of the hen depends upon the number of eggs that they lay. Usually, if the hen is of a good stock and is managed very carefully, she should lay about 100 eggs in one year. Most breeders will produce good eggs for about 3 years.

If the flock is small they may retain the quality of the eggs for almost 4 years. In such cases, the number of eggs laid is drastically small. The breeder will lay about 30 eggs and will then become broody. You need to carefully select the birds for egg production based on the quality of the breed etc. when you are trying to convert it into a lucrative business.

The weight of the eggs laid will be about 45 grams. Fertility is about 80% normally and the hatchability is also approximately the same. The incubation period is usually between 26 to 28 days.

Egg laying in Guinea Fowl may begin when they are only 17 weeks old or earlier in some cases. In the tropical parts of Africa, Guinea Fowl will lay eggs only when the rainy season begins. They will stop a few weeks after that.

A normal clutch size is about 15 eggs. The eggs of Guinea Fowl are much smaller than that of the hens. However, they are considered to be very tasty and nutritious and make for great delicacies in several parts of the world.

The shell is very hard. With of chickens, a method called candling is used to see if the eggs are fertile. The egg is held up against light to see the embryo. This is not easy to do with Guinea Fowl eggs. The hard shells also make it very difficult for you to incubate the eggs artificially.

In temperate parts of the world, the laying season can go up to 40 weeks. Caged birds lay more eggs if they are maintained under the most ideal conditions. They will usually lay about 180 eggs. Out of this at least 150 can be incubated while about 110 will hatch to produce keets. If you have reared your bird intensively and have trained it to lay on the soil, you should be able to get about 70-100 eggs every year. Out of this, 60 of them at least should hatch to produce healthy little keets.

All the details of managing the keets is provided in the previous chapters. You will follow the same guidelines even for the keets that you hatch in your own yard or farm. Just make sure that the temperature and nutritional requirements of the birds are met properly.

Before this, you will have to understand how natural incubation occurs in Guinea Fowl. You will also know what to do if the eggs are abandoned or if you have to intervene because of the death of a parent. Artificial incubation is a challenge with Guinea Fowl eggs and you need to be extremely cautious.

d. Hatching the eggs
You may either allow the Guinea Fowl to incubate and hatch the eggs naturally or may intervene. In several cases, Guinea Fowl will abandon the eggs and wander out after laying the eggs. If you are going to hatch the eggs artificially, collecting them properly is necessary first. In case of normal temperatures, you can collect the eggs four times a day.

However if the temperatures soar above 28 degrees Celsius, you need to make sure that the eggs are collected more often. When the temperatures are too high, the quality of the egg shell diminishes and you will have a lot of trouble incubating the eggs.

If the breeder is stressed by the heat, she may reduce the consumption of food. Consequently, the quality of the egg is also compromised. The weight of the egg will decline drastically. It is idea to store the eggs in a temperature of about 18.5 degree Celsius. The relative humidity needs to be maintained at 80%.

You can obtain humidifiers online to make sure that you are able to provide the necessary amount of moisture for the eggs.

If you do not set the egg for 7 days or more, hatchability decreases as the time of storage increases. There are several other factors that may affect the hatchability of the eggs including the shape of the eggs, the quality of the shell, the size of the egg, the temperature of the incubator etc. If the temperature within the incubator fluctuates too drastically, the eggs will become porous and the hatchability will decline rapidly.

If your breeder flock is younger, you can expect better quality of the eggs. The shell is harder and thicker. But, with each breeding season, the thickness and quality begins to diminish. Eventually, hatchability of the eggs will stop completely. That is why you need to make sure that you do not have the same breeder for more than 3 years if your flock size is considerably larger.

The time when the egg is laid also determines the hatchability. For instance, if the egg is laid early in the morning, it is likely to have poor hatchability. On the other hand, when the egg is laid in the middle of the day, the hatchability of the egg is greater.

e. Incubating the eggs
If the breeder becomes broody, then your eggs will hatch naturally. However, if the breeder abandons the clutch, you will have to artificially incubate the eggs.

Now, when you are artificially incubating the eggs, you need to be very careful about the way you handle the eggs that are going to be hatched. Collect the eggs frequently and make sure that you get rid of any egg that is very dirty and soiled. That is when you can be sure of healthy keets without any unwanted infections that could even spread to the entire flock, that is quite vulnerable at that age.

In case of purebred eggs, the incubation period is between 26 and 28 days, while in case of cross breeds, this number will vary between 24 to 25 days. The method of incubation is the same as any other poultry bird.

Commercially available incubators are good enough for Guinea Fowl. They may come with instructions for Guinea Fowl specifically. In case there are no instructions for these birds, you can even follow the instructions given for pheasants or turkeys. The price of an incubator can range from $100-$1000 or *£50-£500* depending upon the quality and the features.

Now you do not need something too fancy. All you need to ensure with your incubator is that it comes with an automatic turner. If not you will have to manually turn the eggs at regular intervals. A good incubator will also come with humidity settings that can help ensure more hatchability in the eggs. You can buy an incubator online or in any poultry supply store.

For those who own Guinea Fowl, an incubator is almost mandatory to have. You see, when a few of the eggs hatch and the keets begin to move around, the hen will abandon the nest even if many of them have not even hatched yet. You will have to take care of the eggs then. If the eggs are still warm they can be hatched under other broody birds like chickens if you have a mixed coop. When you do this, make sure that the new broody hen that you are putting the eggs under is fully checked for lice and treated accordingly.

If you are using an artificial incubator, it is advised that you keep the temperature at about 37 degree Celsius. Humidity should be maintained at 58%. For the first 24 days, you will have to turn the eggs at least thrice a day. This can be avoided if your incubator comes with an egg turner.

In rare cases of complete natural incubation, this process occurs a few months after the laying season which is typically in April or May. If you are using a chicken to hatch the Guinea Fowl egg, you can hatch about 15 under a Bantam chicken and about 30 under a regular standard sized chicken. It does not matter which form of hatching you opt for, the care that you provide after the keets have arrived is most important.

1. Things you need to keep handy for incubation
In order to incubate the eggs, it is not enough to just have the incubator. There are several things that you need to keep handy to make sure that you do not delay any important step in incubating the egg.

You see, Guinea Fowl eggs have hard shells and are more robust than chicken eggs. However, when it comes to hatching and incubation, they need careful care to make sure that the keets do not have any diseases or deformities when they arrive.

The first thing to do is to study the incubator properly. You need know how your model works and the exact requirements of temperature and humidity for Guinea Fowl eggs. Then, you will have to put together a Guinea Fowl egg incubation kit with the following things:

- A thermometer to check the internal temperature of the incubator.
- Egg sanitizers that you can use to clean the incubator before putting the eggs in.
- Trays or egg boxes in order to place the eggs before you set them.
- Candler to check the progress of the eggs. This is not easy when it comes to guinea eggs because of the hard shell.
- A lead pencil to mark the eggs when you turn them.
- Food coloring that lets you see the water level inside the incubator.
- Sponges or disposable cups to increase humidity inside the incubators.
- Fine grain sandpaper in order to remove any stubborn dirt from a dirty egg.
- Disposable gloves to make sure that the eggs remain sanitized even after handling them several times.
- A water bulb thermometer to check humidity.

- A brooder to keep the keets after they hatch. You may set up the brooder as mentioned in the earlier chapters.
- A feeder
- Water bowl with marbles for the keets that hatch.
- A heat lamp
- Appropriate feed.
- Lining for the brooder
- A cover for the brooder box
- Antibacterial hand soap.

When you have put together this kit, you can take proper care of all your eggs. The only thing you need to remember is that the equipment needs to be checked from time to time. Before you place the eggs inside the incubator, you need to be sure that it is safe to put them in. Plug the machine in and check for the following signs:

- If you have a circulated model, it is necessary for the fan to turn without making any noise. If it is noisy or isn't turning, get it fixed immediately.
- The wafer should not be more than three years old. If it has cracks or other damages, you must replace it.
- If you have a separate egg turner, plug it in to ensure that it is working properly. It should be able to turn equally in both directions. If not, your eggs will not be turned properly and may be severely damaged.
- If you have a digital thermometer, check if it is working properly. Place it in warm water and see if the reading changes. If not, you need to get a new one.
- A wet bulb thermometer must have new wicks. The old ones may have bacterial growth that is harmful for the chicks.

You have to sanitize all the parts of the incubator to prevent any chance of infection in the keets that hatch. They will be highly vulnerable to bacterial and viral infections that can even prove fatal to them. So, be extremely careful.

2. How to wash the eggs before incubation?

Some people may debate that washing the eggs is not the best option for embryo development. However, hygiene is the first thing when it comes to incubating your eggs and ensuring that they produce healthy keets.

The first thing to do would be to wash the eggs gently. Even if an egg looks extremely clean, it could be home to several bacterias. They are potentially hazardous to the entire hatch.

If the eggs are really dirty, don't set them even if you are able to wash them. Some of them will sand the dirt out with sandpaper and still keep the eggs. But, normally, eggs that are very dirty will not hatch. In most cases, the eggs kept near this egg will also fail to hatch.

When washing your eggs make sure that the water is slightly warm. It should be about the same temperature as the palm of your hand. Using a thermometer can help with the accuracy. As you wash, if the water begins to get a little cloudy, change it and continue.

If you use water that is too cold, the egg will shrink from within. In addition to that, any bacterial on the surface will be sucked into the egg. If the water is too hot, the contents will expand. This leads to sticking of the embryo on the shell. When the water is the right temperature, the contents will expand enough to block all the pores that let the bacteria in but not so much that the embryo gets stuck on the wall.

The rule of thumb is to start with the cleanest eggs and then move on to washing the dirtier ones.

You can get an egg sanitizer such as F10 or Tektrol to wash the eggs. Make a solution as per the instructions to make sure that your eggs are safe. You can use this sanitizer not only to clean the eggs but also the different parts of the incubator such as the turner.

You need to make sure that all the eggs are equally cleaned. That means, you need to use the exact same process for each egg. If you are dipping one egg into the solution, do not wash the other under a tap. If you decide to towel dry on egg, make sure that you towel dry all of them. In case you want to incubate eggs that have been laid at different times, you will do so in different incubators. That way, you are certain that all eggs have been cleaned and set in the exact same way.

Sanitizing is one of the most important practices. Even the candler needs to be sanitized whenever it is used to ensure the best health among your keets. Whenever you handle the eggs, make sure you use fresh rubber gloves to prevent any chance of infection or contamination.

When eggs are properly washed and sanitized, the survival rate of the keets increases by 15% at least.

3. Setting up the incubator
Setting up an incubator to ensure the right temperature and humidity requirements is a 9 step process:

1. Make sure that your incubator is in a proper location. It is best that you fix the location of the incubator and avoid moving it around. The best place to keep the incubator is a basement, the closet or a spare room. Avoid places that are humid or warm. You must never place the incubator under direct sunlight or any heat source such as a vent. If there is a door or window or even an air conditioner near the incubator, it may lead to a lot of temperature fluctuations that can harm embryo development. Make sure that the incubator is free from noise, the risk of being bumped by kids or pets etc.

2. To keep the humidity in the incubator, it is important to add water sometimes. You will have a plastic liner that you can add water to. This liner must be placed in the incubator before you pour any water in. Make sure that you only add warm water directly to the base. The base

will have separate sections that can hold water. You need to pick the largest section with no air holes and fill it just up to the brim. Usually this can be a little hard to notice with clear water. That is why it is advisable to add a few drops of food coloring to the water first.

3. Once the water has been added, you will have to place a wire mesh on the base. The edges of the mesh should be clean to make sure that the keets do not get injured. You need to be wary of any sharp edges. They can be covered with cloth if you are unable to repair them.

4. In case you plan to use a turner, this is when you place it in the incubator. Make sure that the turner is functioning properly. You must be able to slide it into place easily. When you force a turner in, it may not turn properly and may damage the whole incubator eventually.

5. You need to make sure that your thermometer is adjusted properly. You must always make sure that your turner is in line with the highest part of your eggs, whether they are kept on the sides or inside an incubator. It is best to find an incubator that already has a clip to place the thermometer in.

6. It is advisable to place a hygrometer inside the incubator. This can measure the humidity inside. It should be in the centre of the incubator and away from the heat source to make sure that it does not show wrong readings.

7. Now, plug the incubator in after ensuring that the wire does not make anyone trip over. If that happens, the incubator may be jerked, damaging the eggs. It may even unplug the incubator accidentally. For homes with pets, you need to tape all the plugs into the socket of the wall.

8. Setting the incubator up a day or two before you place the eggs in makes sure that all the readings are correct. It will

take a few attempts to ensure that the temperature and humidity readings are exactly as required by Guinea Fowl eggs. Even half a degree of deviation from the recommended settings can lead to early or late hatching, leading to deformed keets.

9. Make sure you have an incubation diary. This is not a must have but can really help you learn about the process of incubation and the changes that you need to expect with your next batch. In case you have a poor hatch, you will know exactly what mistakes you made with your eggs. Make sure you note down the date and the time of setting the eggs, the quantity, the turning time and date, adjustments made in temperature or humidity etc.

As soon as the incubator is set, you are ready to place the eggs in and start the process of actually turning them and waiting for them to hatch successfully.

4. Turning the eggs and setting them

As soon as the incubator has been set up and the eggs have been cleaned, the next thing to do is setting the eggs. You have to check a few things before you set the eggs. You already know the incubation period for guinea eggs and how to set the incubator up. The one thing you need to understand is that you need to turn the eggs properly to make sure that they are incubated equally on both sides.

In case of guinea eggs, they will hatch well when you keep them upright. This means that the point of the egg must face downwards and not upwards. If you do it the other way around, the keets also develop upside down and will not be able to break out of the egg.

It is quite simple to set a Guinea Fowl egg. It is related entirely to how you turn the eggs. The turning method varies as per the species of the bird. For example, in case of chickens, ducks or game birds, you need to fulfil certain turning needs. Since Guinea

Fowl fall in the same category, you will follow a few necessary steps. And yes, there is a wrong way of turning eggs.

Guinea eggs must never be turned in a complete circle. When you do this, all the contents inside the egg will get tangled up and will harm the embryo. Instead, you need to keep the egg with the point down and then keep turning it to the left, ensuring that the plane is at 90 degrees. So, basically, you turn the eggs at a 45 degree angle from the centre.

If you have an automatic turner, this will be done for you by the instrument. For those who are unsure of keeping the eggs in an upright position without a turner, you can even turn the eggs keeping them on the sides. If you choose to keep the egg on the side, try to ensure that all the large ends of the eggs face in one direction. Even on the sides, the eggs are slightly tilted, making sure that the air sack remains at the large end. If your eggs roll around a little, don't worry about it too much. You need to be accurate with this.

You need to keep turning the eggs for at least 3 days prior to the completion of the incubation period. Watch the eggs for pipping for the last week. If you do notice any signs that the eggs are going to hatch, stop turning them. When you continue to turn the eggs despite the keets being ready to hatch, you will disorient them and they will be unable to peck their way out. For a guinea egg, the ideal time to stop turning it is when the egg is about 23 days old.

In case you are turning the eggs manually you will have to turn them an odd number of times. You can turn them 3, 5 or 7 times each day. The odd number is crucial to ensure that they same side of the egg is downwards every night. The ideal times to turn the eggs would be as soon as you wake up, just before you go to bed and once in between.

You may even move the eggs around in the tray. That way, they will be able to get different temperature exposure. This is necessary if your incubator does not have a fan.

When we discuss about setting an egg for incubation, the most crucial thing is the position of the egg. You may wonder why this is so important. You see, birds are naturally inclined to turning the eggs when they incubate them. This need for turning has not been completely understood despite extensive research.

Some reasons for the need to turn the eggs is to make sure that the mortality rate in the eggs will come down. This also prevents any mal positioning in the embryos. In addition to that, you will not have to worry about any retardation in the development of the embryos.

When you turn the eggs regularly, you also ensure that the embryo does not stick to the shell. It remains in the centre, and hence also remains fuller. Vein growth in the embryo is also even and the rate of organ development increases. The nutrients can be easily absorbed by the embryo and the amount of oxygen supplied to the developing keet increases. This way, you are ensured stronger and better developed keets.

Whether you are manually turning the eggs, using a manual turner or even an automatic one, it is necessary to keep an eye on the eggs. If there are any cracks, bad odors or seepage, they should be immediately discarded.

Some people will try to keep the cracked eggs in the incubator if they are not severely damaged. But, you need to understand that these eggs will not be able to retain any moisture. They will eventually spread infections to the other eggs in the incubator.

Seeping eggs must immediately be removed. These eggs will have sticky or fizzy substances that is clearly not water. If there is any bad odor inside the incubator, make sure you find the source. If it is any of the eggs, toss it out immediately. These eggs are rotten and will generally not have a growing embryo within them. Instead, there are chances that these eggs will explode right in the incubator, infecting all the other eggs. This is also quite disgusting for you to clean up.

Disposing the eggs should also be done very carefully. You need to wrap them in plastic or several layers of plastic before you throw them out in the bin. If not, there are chances that you will attract predators like weasels and racoons that are harmful to your eggs.

5. Cleaning the incubator

Besides keeping the eggs clean, you also need to ensure that the incubator is well maintained in order to have a good hatch. Here are a few simple tips to help you keep your incubator clean:

- It does not matter if your incubator is new or has been borrowed. You need to make sure that you clean it after one hatch is over. This will keep it clean for the next one. Germs and dust will remain in the incubator causing problems despite taking good care of the eggs. Make sure that the incubator is cleaned 2 days before you place the eggs in.
- Clean the incubator with a disinfectant such as Clorox. You will need about 4 parts of warm water and one part of the disinfectant. Soak all the parts of your incubator in this solution for about 10 minutes. All the electrical parts must be removed before you do this. Wipe these parts down with clean water and if there is any stubborn dirt, use a new toothbrush to clean it. Wafers can also be cleaned with a soft toothbrush.
- After the keets have hatched, remove all the shells from the incubator. Then follow the same cleaning method as mentioned above.

Make sure that your incubator is dried completely after each cleaning session. That keeps it free from unwanted microbes.

Chapter 7: Common Guinea Fowl Diseases

Guinea Fowl are hardy birds that are able to fight most diseases. However, they are also susceptible to the diseases that affect any common poultry birds like turkeys and chickens. There are two broad categories of diseases in the case of poultry birds- Respiratory diseases and Non Respiratory diseases. The former affect the respiratory system while the latter could be metabolic or nutritional in nature. With birds, you need to be most careful of infections spread by fungi, bacteria, virus and protozoans.

a. Signs of illnesses in Guinea Fowl

When you have a large flock of guinea hen, you need to make sure that you keep an eye on your birds to check for any signs of disease. You will not ignore even the slightest changes in the physical appearance or behavior of the birds as it may put the whole flock at risk of contracting a certain disease. Here are some tips to check if your bird is in good health or not:

Check the head
The head of the bird is the best give away for any sickness or disease. Most poultry diseases will have symptoms associated with the head. The common signs are liquid discharge from the nostrils and the eyes of the bird which is a sign of some respiratory disorder. The face may swell, including the wattles, showing that your bird has some serious infection.

Normally, a bird who is unwell will stop eating and drinking. Other sure shot signs of disease and infection are dullness in the eyes, redness in the tear ducts and constant sneezing. If you see that one of the birds is behaving strangely, check the head first to confirm any form of infection or metabolic disease.

The body
Normally, when birds fall sick, the first thing to be affected is breathing. Birds begin to have very labored breathing that is accompanied by a rattling sound. When this happens, get your

95

bird checked by a vet immediately. Then, run your fingers over the body of the bird. If you feel that the bird is emaciated, then it is a sign of sickness. This happens mostly when the consumption of water lowers, leading to dehydration. In some cases, the abdomen of the bird becomes very enlarged. Also, a bird that is sick will be seated in a hunching position and will puff up the feathers frequently.

Look at the cloaca
The vent beneath the tail is called the cloaca. This is one of the most important sites of infection if the bird is not kept clean. There could be mites around this region accompanied by redness and swelling. This is an indication of parasites that are making the bird sick. The feathers in this area should not be soiled and stuck together. If they are, then it is a sign of diarrhoea or even a pasty vent syndrome.

When a bird is sick, the common tendency is to pick the feathers around the vent. This leads to sores and wounds that the bird will continue to pick at. In case of hens you can even examine the eggs that are laid. If the eggs are rough, have soft shells or even absent shells in some cases, it is a sign of illness in your bird.

Weakness
If your bird is always sitting and shows a lot of resistance towards standing, then there are chances that he has some infection in the foot. The knees of the bird will look extremely weak and the bird will really struggle to walk around. The legs of the bird may become pale and look inflamed and sore. Normally, Guinea Fowl will sit with the legs drawn towards the body. If the bird sits with the legs spread out in front of him, he is most probably not in the best of health.

Besides this, you may even notice that your bird smells fowl or looks really untidy. Unfortunately, in most cases, Guinea Fowl do not show very evident symptoms of disease and may just succumb to the infection. It is your job as the keeper to make sure that you watch out for these signs. If you notice any illness in one of the birds, it is a good idea to isolate him immediately till you get him checked by a vet. That way you can prevent the disease from spreading to the other birds in the flock as well. Keep the sick bird in a warm area, free from any drafts and consult your vet immediately.

b. Respiratory illnesses

The common respiratory illnesses are:

Fowl Pox

This disease has a dry form and a wet form. When dry you will notice several scabs or wart like developments on areas without feathers. Removing these scabs leads to profuse bleeding. In the wet form, you will see several lesions in the pharynx, larynx, trachea and the mouth. The latter is caused due to any obstruction in the respiratory passage.

This is a viral infection that is normally transmitted by mosquitoes. It spreads very slowly and is mostly incurable. Vaccination is available to prevent the condition. In addition to that, you can also keep the coop free from mosquitoes to prevent any transmission.

Newcastle disease

This condition is very contagious and is lethal. The internal organs are normally affected with this condition. It can even spread to people and other mammals. The disease can be mild, moderate or severe. In the initial stages, you will see that the chirps of the keets get hoarse, they will have discharge from the nostrils, breathing is labored, the face swells, paralysis occurs and trembling occurs too.

In adult birds, feeding and drinking reduces drastically. This is an airborne disease that usually spreads when you walk around the coop with contaminated shoes. It can also be passed in to the egg in which case the embryo will die before hatching.

There is no specific treatment for this condition either. You can provide a cycle of antibiotics in the mild to moderate stage. For chicks, increasing temperature by 5 degrees is usually helpful. Good sanitation and vaccination can help prevent the condition.

Avian influenza
This condition affects all birds. It can either be mild or severe. In case of the mild form of the disease, the common symptoms include sudden loss of appetite, heavy breathing, diarrhoea, and low mortality among hatchlings. When it is severe, the face swells and extreme dehydration may occur. Blood is discharged from the nostrils. Eggs are usually soft shelled or the birds may not lay eggs at all.

This is a viral disease that is spread through the manure. It can be controlled by keeping the surroundings of the bird clean and free from any dirt or contamination. Some rodents may transmit this condition too.

Proper nutrition, good husbandry and preventive vaccines are the only treatment options for this condition. These are only preventive measures. Only in the mild form can this condition be cured with medication and care.

Infectious Coryza
This condition is also known as roup. The common clinical symptoms include foul smelling discharge from the nose and the eyes, troubled breathing and swelling around the face of the bird. Sometimes, the eyelids stick together. Diarrhoea is also common. While birds do not exactly die from coryza, it is possible that the egg production decreases. In addition to that they may even be more susceptible to other infectious diseases.

This condition is always transmitted from one bird to another. Respiratory droplets in the air can carry this disease too. Several water soluble antibiotics can be administered to the bird. Some of these medicines can only be administered to birds that are 14 weeks old at least.

Good sanitation is the best way to prevent this condition from spreading. Mixing flocks can also lead to the transmission of this condition.

Chlamydiosis

This is another condition that will affect most birds. It can affect human beings too. Chickens are most susceptible to this condition among poultry birds. Among avians, parrots are most susceptible, giving the condition the name 'parrot fever'

Birds affected with this condition will have discharge from the eyes and the nose, sudden weight loss, conjunctivitis, weakness, sinusitis and reduced appetite. The condition is transmitted through dirty shoes or even clothes. Even birds that have recovered from the condition will remain potential carriers. If there is any environmental stress, the disease can recur.

Treatment includes chlorotetracycline that is administered for about 3 weeks. There are several other antibiotics that have proven to be effective against chlamydiosis too. When you administer any medicine to your flock, make sure you follow the FDA guidelines very strictly.

Swollen head syndrome

Also known as facial cellulitis, this condition affects almost all poultry birds except geese and ducks. Initially, sneezing is seen among birds. This is followed by reddening of the eyes and the tear ducts. The entire region of the face including the wattles will swell. In addition to this, you may observe twisting of the neck and disorientation in birds that are severely affected.

It can spread when one bird comes in contact with another infected bird. It is caused by a virus that is known as pneumovirus and there is no real treatment process that can help the bird. You can try prescribed antibiotic treatments in the initial stages of the condition.

Aspergillosis

This condition is also known as brooder pneumonia or fungal pneumonia. It is a very acute disease when it affects younger birds and most often leads to death. Birds will have great difficulty breathing and will also almost stop eating. Paralysis and convulsions may also occur in birds due to toxins of the fungi.

In adult birds, a twisted neck, bluish color of the skin and strained breathing is quite common. They may also have nervous disorders in severe conditions. The condition is usually spread by a virus that thrives well in damp and warm conditions. Room temperature or temperatures slightly higher than that are good enough for the virus to spread. Normally, transmission of the disease occurs through contaminated water and food.

Improving ventilation and maintaining clean conditions in the coop is the best way to prevent the condition from spreading. The brooding area, especially, needs to be cleaned at regular intervals. Do not leave any dirty litter in the coop. While you do not have to clean it out so often in case of Guinea Fowl, you need to be very careful about letting it get too dirty.

c. Non Respiratory illnesses
The non-respiratory illnesses have several categories including:

1. Viral Infections
These conditions are usually non reversible and can be very severe in birds. Viruses thrive mostly in areas that are damp and dirty. Some of the common viral infections of Guinea Fowl include:

Lymphoid leucosis
The incubation of this virus is about 4 weeks. Therefore initial signs are not very obvious. Only after 16 weeks will you be able to see any symptoms. By this time, you will see that the birds have started to become very weak. The comb and the wattles do not develop properly. The abdomen is enlarged and the droppings are greenish in color.

Usually, this condition affects keets and is transmitted through the egg. In case of mature birds, the condition spreads from one bird to the other. It cannot be transmitted through air. The best way to prevent this condition is to ensure that the birds that are chosen for laying are free from this condition. A few tests will help a vet determine whether the brooder is a carrier or not. There is no treatment and will usually lead to death in the birds.

Equine encephalitis

You must not confuse this condition with St. Louis Encephilitis. Both conditions are transmitted by mosquitoes. However, they are clinically very different.

This disease is contagious among birds and can also affect mammals like horses. Sometimes, it may even affect people. The common symptoms are reduced food consumption, paralysis and even staggering. The birds that survive will become blind and may even have paralysis of the muscles. Common signs are difficulty in holding the head up. Mortality rates are very high with infected birds.

Only preventive measures such as keeping the area free from weed can be taken. You must also prevent any mosquitos in the coop of your birds. Vaccines can also be provided.

Avian encephalomyelitis

This disease will occur in the first week of the bird's life. The chicks that are affected will become very lethargic and will show tremors in the head and neck and complete incoordination eventually. In adult birds, the egg production drops and the consumption of food and water reduces too. The birds that have recovered are not a threat usually.

However, when young birds are infected, they are normally removed or euthanized because they will eventually meet a very painful end. Vaccinations are available but the condition cannot be treated.

Egg drop syndrome

This condition can affect the birds without any symptoms or signs. You will only notice these symptoms after the eggs have been laid. The eggs are extremely fragile with thin shells. Sometimes, the shell may be missing altogether. Diarrhoea is normally observed in birds that have this condition.

This condition was first introduced into chickens through a vaccine that was contaminated. It was then passed down the generations. Other species developed this condition due to contact with feces of birds that were already infected. Good husbandry and nutrition are the only preventive measures that you can take against these conditions.

2. Bacterial Infections

Bacterial infections are the most common type of infections in birds. Some diseases that you will commonly observe include:

Fowl cholera

This is a condition that affects most poultry birds. It will only strike birds after they are 6 weeks of age. When it is acute, the condition spreads so fast that the bird will die before you notice any symptoms. If it is still mild and on the onset, you will observe conditions like labored breathing, diarrhoea, infections in the joints, untidy feathers and even loss of weight. As the condition progresses, the bird will develop several abscesses on the feet and the wattles.

This condition is commonly transmitted by new birds in the flock, wild birds, rodents and predators. The condition, when diagnosed, can be treated using sulfa drugs. The birds can also be vaccinated to ensure that they do not contract the disease in the first place.

Pullorum or Bacillary White Diarrhoea

This condition will most often affect chickens and turkeys. Other birds like Guinea Fowl are susceptible too. The only birds that are usually not affected are game birds like pheasants when they are commercially grown.

When this condition affects young birds, it will lead to death within 7 days of contraction. If they survive they will remain carriers of the condition throughout. The common clinical signs of this condition include weakness, diarrhoea, droopiness and a pasted vent. The birds are normally stunted because they are unable to consume any food.

This condition is normally transmitted from the hen to the egg. If you have contaminated incubators, chick boxes, houses and other equipment, the infection will become more severe over time. It is also possible that this condition is transmitted through the food consumed by the birds.

You can provide various antibacterial medicines and sulfonamides to prevent this condition from affecting your flock. It is not possible to eradicate the disease. If your flock is infected, you need to eradicate the whole flock as per the law. You will contact the corresponding federal agency to take care of the issue. In some poultry shows you need to obtain a "pollurum free" certificate for your flock in order to enter them.

Ulcerative enteritis
This condition affects Guinea Fowl, geese, partridges and turkeys most commonly. This condition is acute and the survival of the affected bird is a very slim chance. The bird will usually die before the symptoms are detected. In case the infection is not acute, you will see symptoms like reduced food consumption and depression among the birds. The birds assume a humped sitting position and will keep their eyes closed most of the time. Watery droppings and ruffled feathers are among the other symptoms of this condition.

Normally, the birds are only affected when they come in contact with a bird carrying the condition. It can also be transmitted through the feces of these birds. The infection can be carried on to the other members of the flock through your shoes and clothes and even rodents. Feed bags are the most common growth sites for these bacteria.

You can use a combination of bacitracin and neomycin to control the condition. There are several other antibiotics that your vet will be able to recommend for your bird including penicillin. This condition can only be prevented by keeping the coop extremely clean and disinfected.

Botulism
This is a condition that can even affect human beings and other mammals. The only animal that is resistant to this condition is the turkey vulture. The disease is normally caused by the

consumption of foods that are contaminated. The bacteria *Clostridium botulini* is responsible for this condition. Paralysis is the most common symptom in Guinea Fowl just a few hours after eating the food that is contaminated. Although the birds are mentally alert, they are paralyzed below the neck. Even the feathers on the neck become loose, exposing the follicles.

In case the bird has consumed a lot of the contaminated food, death will occur in 24 hours or lesser. The birds usually die because the respiratory organs become paralyzed. If the amount of food consumed is not lethal, the bird will display extreme sleepiness and fatigue.

This disease is only spread through organic matter including dead birds around the coop. It can be carried by maggots and other insects too. It doesn't normally spread from one bird to another.

You need to remove the spoiled food immediately. If there are any dead birds in the coop, clear them out instantly. Then you need to flush the while flock by adding Epsom salts to the water. Potassium permanganate when added to water can also help treat the condition effectively. Your vet should also be able to provide your bird with an antitoxin medicine or injection.

To prevent the condition, keep flies and pests away. Make sure that you replace food even if you have the slightest suspicion against it. You must also replace the feed every day to prevent any contamination or infection.

Staphylococcus
This bacteria will affect all poultry birds. There are three forms of infection- bumblefoot, acute or septicaemia and chronic or arthritic. The acute form of the condition leads to sudden loss of appetite, fever, listlessness and discomfort during movement. These symptoms are similar to fowl cholera. The eggs may also have bad rot. The feces of the bird will be very watery and the joints are swollen. Productivity of the birds will drop when they are infected.

In case of the arthritic form, you will see lameness in the birds. You may also see blisters on the breast. Whenever they move, the birds will display great discomfort and symptoms of pain. They will be reluctant to walk and would most likely want to sit instead of standing.

Bumblefoot is a localized condition. It is caused by any injury or puncture in the foot. The foot pads become swollen and the bird is very hesitant to walk or stand. There is a lot of obvious pain during movement.

This condition is soil borne. You will normally see an outbreak in a flock after a storm or rain. When your free range Guinea Fowl drink from still water in the puddles, the bacterial infection occurs. Treatment includes addition of Novobiocin in the feed for a total of 7 days. You may also add Erythromycin in the water or the feed for about 5 days. Preventing the condition is possible by isolating birds that are infected. You can also provide a balanced meal to keep your flock protected. Removing any object that could lead to injuries in the foot is the best way to prevent bumblefoot.

In order to prevent any disease and to control the condition when it affects the birds, you need a good veterinarian. The next section tells you all about finding a good vet to support you in your journey or raising guineas.

d. Behavioral problems in Guinea Fowl
It has commonly been observed that birds in captivity develop several abnormalities in their behaviour. This includes any poultry birds or even exotic pets. Some of the common Guinea Fowl behavioural problems are:

Feather pecking
This is a common behavioral issue with birds that are reared for their eggs. You will see that they begin to peck the feathers of other birds in the flock. This can either be gentle or extremely severe. If feather pecking in your flock is gentle, it is not a cause for worry. However, when the pecking becomes painful leading to

bleeding or bruises, it could be a sign of possible cannibalism and could even lead to death. This can be caused by various factors including poor husbandry, sudden changes in the diet of the bird and genetics. You can control this by selectively breeding birds that are healthier. In order to reduce the intensity of feather pecking, it is recommended that you trim the beaks of your Guinea Fowl.

Cannibalism

Sometimes, Guinea Fowl may begin to consume parts of their flock mates or may even eat an entire bird. This commonly happens when birds are reared for egg production. Usually this is preceded by severe feather pecking, leading to sudden decline in the size of the flock. It has been noticed that chicks that have been naturally incubated have a lower chance of resorting to cannibalism than the ones artificially incubated.

The common control methods include beak trimming, selective breeding, installing perches and even providing birds with blinders. You must not include new birds to a flock where cannibalism is prevalent as the new members will learn this behavior very easily in order to fit in.

Vent pecking

This condition is commonly known as cloacal cannibalism. The birds tend to peck the feathers around the cloaca, leading to damage in the underlying tissue or the skin in that region. Birds may peck their own feathers or the feathers of other birds. This type of pecking leads to increased susceptibility towards diseases. Using dim lights in the nesting boxes, changing the diet too often and using a drinker that the birds are unable to use properly can lead to vent picking. This commonly indicates some sort of stress in the bird.

Polydipsia

Polydypsia means a sudden increase in the consumption of water. It is usually a sign of toxic ingestion in birds or may even indicate too much consumption of certain foods. If you give your Guinea Fowl too many table scraps, salt toxicity is possible. Sometimes polydipsia may occur as a symptom of some other disease such as liver or renal disease, Vitamin deficiency etc.

e. Veterinary Care

It is quite a challenge to find a good veterinarian who can provide adequate care for your guineas. The issue with these birds is that they are not exotic birds like parrots but need more specialized care than other pets like dogs and cats. There are some who mainly specialize in poultry but finding them can be a challenge.

In an emergency, it is alright if you look for a vet who treats any species of animals as he is able to provide the first aid that your bird needs. However, your regular vet should have experience with poultry birds so that he can provide timely vaccinations and assistance to your flock.

Now if you want to look for a vet that specializes in poultry, you can ask a local vet or feed store. Even your department of agriculture can help you with that. A directory of all registered poultry vets is available on www.chickenvet.com. This website can provide not only the directory but also a lot of ongoing education about the veterinary care that is being given to poultry birds like Guinea Fowl.

In any case, finding a good vet for poultry is quite a challenge. There is also a lot of ignorance on the part of the poultry keepers when it comes to understanding poultry vets. They believe that most vets are not qualified enough to treat their birds. The fact is that poultry vets do a lot of research about the different birds, subscribe to specialized magazines, look for reliable online resources and stay in touch with all the recent trends in poultry medicine. Of course, there are others who will simply inject your birds with a series of antibiotics and not take any responsibility for the health of the bird.

In fact, very few treatments are licensed for vets to use on birds like Guinea Fowl. These medicines also do not come in quantities that are feasible for small scale owners and backyard breeders. The limited resources available on the market make it a lot more important for you to find a good poultry vet who can take care of the birds well and make sure that they do not contract diseases that do not have licensed treatment options. He should also be aware of alternatives should the bird contract the disease through unknown sources or poor husbandry.

Now, if you find a vet who does not think that Guinea Fowl require that much care, you may think that he is right. After all they are known for being so hardy and resistant to diseases. However, what you really need to know is that like any bird, even your guinea is susceptible to several diseases. The worst thing about birds that live in flocks is that the disease spreads from one bird to another before you can even realize. If your vet makes you feel like it is actually quite strange that you are taking too much care of your Guinea Fowl, you need to find another one.

When you go to a vet, ask him the following questions:

1. What is the general opinion about keeping guineas as pets?
If the vet finds it strange that you would opt for a Guinea Fowl as your companion, then he will definitely not be able to relate to your need for providing that much care to the bird. You will find it hard to work with a vet who treats your beloved pets as commercially raised birds. It is best that you find someone who understands that guineas can make wonderful pets and that their health is as important to the owner as the health of another common pet like a dog or a cat.

2. How often does he or she treat bird like the Guinea Fowl?
It is quite common for regular vets to treat poultry birds. That is alright if he or she has some experience with poultry birds. You see when they study medicine, most vets have to spend a few hours learning about poultry birds and working with them. Then, they can either have a specialization in these birds or can improve their knowledge through regular practice. If the vet sees at least 2-3 poultry birds every day, he may have the experience that is needed to deal with birds like the Guinea Fowl.

3. Do they normally perform surgeries on these birds? What kind?

There are several surgical requirements of birds such as removal of tumors, correction of certain feet and beak deformities etc. If your vet is only into surgical pinioning, it may not be enough for your bird. You also need to make sure that they have a facility to house birds after surgery. In addition to that, your vet must provide 24 hour emergency services or should be able to recommended a reliable emergency care service.

4. Are they familiar with all the right doses of antibiotics?

When asked this question, your vet must reply with weight related ratios. If they are not able to tell you what the right dose is for a bird of a certain weight, it means that he is not familiar with it. Antibiotic doses are only effective when given in the right amount and a good poultry vet should be familiar with that.

5. What is their opinion on Superlorin implants?

This is one of the latest treatments used in egg peritonitis treatment. You need to ask these questions to make sure that your vet is well aware of the trends in bird care and management. You can also ask him or her how they keep themselves updated about the various trends in bird care and treatment.

Guinea Fowl fact: Veterinary care is the largest investment when it comes to caring for Guinea Fowl. You will spend close to $10-15 or £7-12 per bird per sitting. Of course this will increase as the flock size decreases. If you have 12 birds, for instance, you will end up spending close to $100 or £50 every time you visit the vet.

f. First Aid and Preventive Care

When you have birds in a flock, injuries cannot be prevented. Sometimes, there may be squabbles and fights within the group leading to cuts and injuries. Birds may end up with broken wings as a result of predator attacks. You need to be able to stop bleeding or keep the wing in place until you are able to take your bird to the vet. This requires a handy first aid kit that has all the supplies that you may require in case there is some emergency including:

- A small bottle with medical saline water to wash off any wound sites.
- Betadine to kill any germs
- Neosporin which is a triple antibiotic
- Nurtidrench to provide vitamins to distressed birds
- Benadryl for keets in order to take care of any wasp, bee or scorpion stings.
- Electrolytes and vitamins to restore the water levels in very hot conditions.
- Honey as a natural antiseptic
- Epsom salt to soak the feet of the birds in case of any splinters. This can also help get rid of any toxins that are causing intestinal blockage in the birds.
- Petroleum jelly or coconut oil to apply on the feet in order to prevent frost bite.
- Styptic pencil or blood stop powder to clot blood. You can also make use of corn starch.
- Gauze pads
- Scissors
- Vet Wrap
- Cotton
- Small syringes or droppers to wash delicate parts like the eye
- Toenail clippers to trim the nails of the birds
- Tweezers to handle small bandages and tapes required by these birds.
- Rubber gloves to protect yourself.
- Small flashlight to examine the bird thoroughly.

You need to keep all these supplies handy and easily available. One of the best options is to put them all in a large and sturdy plastic box with a strong lid. You also need to make a note of all the emergency numbers including your vet and keep it in the box so that you have easy access when required.

Examine this box from time to time to make sure that none of the contents have become dirty and unhygienic. Keep it in a place that is easily accessible to you and the rest of your family members.

Educating yourself about the various accidents that can occur gives you the knowledge that you need to take care of your birds properly. Make sure that other members in your family are also in the loop to help out when you are not around. First aid is extremely important and can save your bird's life at times. It is a good idea to meet your poultry vet and learn a few common first aid practices.

Guinea Fowl fact: When choosing antibiotics, never choose one that may end in 'cane' or 'caine' such as novacaine, lidociane etc. these antibiotics are normally harmful for your bird. In some cases, it can even be fatal to poultry and should always be avoided in your home.

1. Preventive care
In most cases, the only way to safeguard your bird from deadly diseases is to take all the possible preventive measures. Some of the most important preventive measures against diseases include:

Vaccinating your bird
There are several vaccines that are available to prevent the onset of infections. You need to make sure that your bird gets the right dose of antibiotics at the right age to prevent any diseases. You can speak to your vet to decide the different cycles and schedule appointments accordingly.

Good Husbandry
Keeping the coop clean and the birds well-nourished is a part of good husbandry. This makes sure that none of the common virus or bacteria are able to thrive in your bird's natural environment. Giving your birds a well-balanced meal will ensure that they do not contract any disease that is related to lack of certain nutrients. It will also keep the immunity of the bird high.

Keep them active

If you are going to keep your birds indoors, you need to make sure that they have enough space to move around. Guinea Fowl that are kept in a very small enclosure are very stressed and can contract infections quite easily. You also need to make sure that the birds are able to free range and get as much physical and mental stimulation as they need.

Keep red mites away

You can buy special red mite powder from most pet supply stores. Make sure that you dust your birds and also their nests with this powder to prevent diseases. It is a good idea to carry out this dusting every month.

Make sure they have lots of clean water

Birds need clean water to thrive. You need to make sure that the water is free from any possible contamination by changing it on a daily basis. You can also make the water a lot more beneficial to the bird by adding a few drops of apple cider vinegar 3-5 times a week. This keeps the gut of the bird healthy. You also get water soluble antibiotics that can help prevent most diseases.

Take good care of keets

When your birds are younger, they need a lot of care and attention. Make sure that they get the right amount of proteins for proper development. In addition to that, they also need the right amount of light and heat in order to grow without any sort of stress.

Quarantine new birds

Sometimes new birds that are included in a flock may carry several diseases. If you introduce the bird without any quarantining, you are putting the whole flock at risk. Instead it is a good idea to keep the new bird away for 30 days and introduce him only when you are sure of his health.

With these preventive care tips, you should be able to make sure that your birds are healthy. Maintain this and also consult your vet to improve the standards of care for your birds. You are definitely going to be able to raise a healthy flock if you do so.

g. Insurance for Guinea Fowl

Normally, insurance may not be available for Guinea Fowl in particular. You may, however, prepare for medical emergencies by opting for livestock insurance that offers some cover for most poultry. It is advisable that you invest in insurance in order to deal with unexpected health issues effectively. Many poultry owners do not opt for this type of insurance because they believe that it is too expensive. However, the fact remains that having your flock insured can give you a lot of assurance when there is some emergency.

A standard insurance policy for livestock will cover most poultry birds, goats, sheep, pigs, cattle horses and even crocodiles depending on the part of the world that you live in. You can claim insurance in case of any illness, accident, epidemics etc. Some policies may also offer insurance against the death of birds in case of a drought or famine. This is applicable only for certain zones and you need to make sure you check it thoroughly.

You can also claim insurance against thefts. In that case, you need to meet the standard security guidelines listed by the company that you have bought insurance from. Intentional slaughter of the bird is obviously not covered. Some insurance policies may even cover conditions like congenital infertility. You can also claim insurance for accident or loss due to overseas transfer.

For birds like Guinea Fowl, the insurance policy is normally valid after the birds have reached a certain age. This may vary quite drastically and you need to check with your insurance company. The cover may be offered for a year, which you need to renew. When it comes to poultry or livestock, it is a good idea to seek advice from your vet about the best insurance policies for your bird.

How does insurance work?

The insurance policies are quite simple to understand. You will pay a fixed premium to the insurer. Then you will be issued an insurance policy. This will give you all the details such as the period of the insurance cover and the risks that the insurance covers. You will also receive in writing the compensation that you can claim in case of any loss.

If you face a loss, you will lodge a complaint for the amount that you are entitled to. If all the conditions stated in the policy are met, you should be able to get your money.

The value of your Guinea Fowl is calculated based on the quality of the breed, the productivity of your bird and the market value of your bird. When you claim loss, illness or death, you will need to get a certificate from the veterinarian. In case of dead birds, a post mortem report is mandatory too. Only when you prove loss will you be able to claim the full value promised to you in the policy.

You will normally pay between 3.24 to 5.5% of the value of all your birds every year as insurance. Some insurance companies, such as APA insurance, may even insert a small device in the flock which helps trace the bird when needed. They work on radio signals and will be taken back when your vet confirms death of the bird. This is a very active measure that is being taken in order to prevent any fraud or claims that are filed even for livestock that are uninsured. Some policies may even use tags that can be removed quite easily. That way, people can truly benefit from insurance policies.

Why get insurance?

Insurance has several advantages as far as your Guinea Fowl husbandry practice is concerned. The benefits of insurance are:

You can restock your flock in case of severe losses due to droughts. This is very beneficial to people who commercially raise Guinea Fowl.

In case of any climatic risk or difficult period for your flock, you can even use your insurance policy as a collateral. Some of these companies make arrangements for you to obtain financial assistance from certain institutions to obtain food and medicine for your birds.

Most of the veterinary costs may be covered in case of an emergency.

If you do not want to purchase insurance, you need to have some back up funds to deal with an emergency. You could opt for opening a savings account that you put aside some money every month in. That way, you are prepared to take care of unexpected expenses.

Conclusion

Thank you for reading this book. We hope that most of your queries about raising Guinea Fowl have been answered by us. Remember, Guinea Fowl care is progressive and there is no such thing as too much information. Try to subscribe to relevant magazines and online newsletters to improve your knowledge about the bird. You can even speak to your vet for additional tips on keeping your bird healthy and content.

All the information in this book is a compilation of experiences of Guinea Fowl owners. The idea was to make the tips as practical as possible to make the journey less overwhelming for new Guinea Fowl owners. All the information is backed by extensive research to give you the best possible insight into the world of guineas. If you think that this book has been informative, please leave a comment so that other people interested in raising these wonderful birds may be benefited too.

References

The Internet is full of great information for Guinea Fowl keepers. You need to keep yourself updated at all times to make sure that you know what is going on with your fowl. You also need to know about the recent trends in Guinea Fowl rearing in order to provide them with optimal health care. Here are some websites that you can use as references when you need more information about your Guinea Fowl.

Note: at the time of printing, all the websites below were working. As the internet changes rapidly, some sites might no longer live when you read this book. That is, of course, out of our control.

www.homestead.org

www.poultrykeeper.com

www.superforty.com

www.guineas.com

www.efowl.com

www.pets4homes.co.uk

www.guineafarm.com

www.wikihow.com

www.dogbreedinfo.com

www.modernfarmer.com

www.motherearthnews.com

www.nafis.go.ke

www.backyardchickens.com

www.web.uconn.edu

www.forum.backyardpoultry.com

www.chickens.allotment-garden.org

www.guinea-fowl.co.uk

www.raising-guineas.com

www.articles.extension.org

www.guineafowl.com

www.petfinder.com

www.gracelikestogarden.com

www.backyardchickencoops.com.au

www.guineafarm.com

www.poultrykeeperforum.com

www.countrysidenetwork.com

www.bigrunwolfranch.org

www.inpractice.bmj.com

www.business.qld.gov.au

www.poultryhub.org

www.edis.ifas.ufl.edu

References

www.thepoultryguide.com

www.homesteadingtoday.co

www.poultryclub.org

www.rma.usda.gov

www.poultryhelp.com

www.poulvet.com

Made in the USA
Middletown, DE
17 April 2022

64404433R00070